SIX YEARS IN INDIA

SIX YEARS IN INDIA

Or, Sketches of India and Its People, as Seen by a Lady Missionary

BY

MRS. E. J. HUMPHREY

GYAN

ISBN : 978-81-212-1796-5(HB)

First Published, 1866

Published, 2018

Published by

Gyan Publishing House
5, Ansari Road
Daryaganj, New Delhi-110002
Phone: 011-47034999, 9811692060
www.gyanbooks.com
E-mail: books@gyanbooks.com

Printed at: G. Print Process, Delhi.

Printing Office, etc., at Bareilly.

INTRODUCTION.

THE vast peninsula of Hindoostan is located near the center of the Eastern Hemisphere. It is bounded on the north by the Himalaya Mountains, on the east by Burmah and the Bay of Bengal, on the south by the Indian Ocean, on the west by the Arabian sea, Afghanistan, and Beloochistan.

The name Hindoostan signifies literally the place, that is the country, of the Hindoos, *stan* simply signifying place or locality. In like manner Afghanistan signifies the country of the Afghans.

Hindoostan is a magnificent country. Its vast area of one and a half millions of square miles contains every variety of scenery and climate. There are long ranges of lofty mountains, some of which are of immense height and covered with perpetual snows; and large rivers, which irrigate extensive valleys and plains. On these prairie-like plains snows never fall. During the entire year they are clothed with verdure.

No fences or walls divide the land into farms. In the center of each section or township of from two to six hundred acres, stands a village where the farmers live, and from which they go out and till their small fields.

Probably the chief reason of this practice is the tenure on which the lands are held, which precludes the ownership of the farms by the farmers. The lands are all held by the British government, except some small states which native nobles are allowed to retain on condition of fealty to the Queen of England. They are leased in townships by the government to Zamindars, who sub-lease them in small parcels to the farmers. Consequently, the country is dotted with large cities and multitudinous villages.

The houses of the poorer classes are built of sun-dried brick and are thatched with straw; but the nobles and native gentry have dwellings of kiln-dried brick, ornamented with arched verandahs and frescoed ceilings. They are generally, however, entirely destitute of glass, doors, and windows, and, except in the case of the houses of those who have something of an English education, they are wholly without chairs, and tables, and the other articles of furniture which we deem so indispensable. A few brass dishes, a kettle or two, an iron plate on which to bake their chappattees, or graham bread, one or two hookahs or pipes, two or three light bedsteads (charpoys) covered with woven cords, constitute the usual array of household goods.

The people usually build their houses in quadrangular form, with a wide entrance to a courtyard in the center of the building. In this courtyard there are usually a well and a few shade trees, and there they usually sit and smoke their hookahs, and sometimes sleep and take their meals. In the older cities, like Lucknow, Delhi, Agra, etc., there are noble structures—temples, mausoleums, and palaces—the remains of past grandeur, power, and oppression.

The population of the country is reckoned at about two hundred millions.

"But little is known of the first inhabitants of the country. The Bheels of Central India, the Gonds of Nerbudda, and some of the tribes of the Himalayas, are supposed to be their descendants.

"The next settlers were the Hindoos, who are of the Indo-Germanic family. Bodies of this people went off to the west from Central Asia, and settled in Europe. The Germans and English are descendants of this great shepherd race. Other bands passed into the plains of the

Indus and gradually subdued the tribes of Scythian descent, and spread themselves over the whole country."

The Hindoos are well formed and athletic, with regular features and oval faces like Europeans. In some sections of the country, where they subsist largely upon rice, they are weaker and more effeminate.

The history of India is divided into three parts: the Hindoo, Mohammedan, and Christian. The history of the Hindoo period is extremely vague. We have no reliable information concerning the dynasties that rose and fell. It is clear, however, from memorials that remain, and upon which we can rely, that civilization and literature of a certain kind flourished in ages long since past. The people made important discoveries in several branches of science, particularly in mathematics and astronomy.

The Hindoos invented the decimal system of notation. Many centuries ago they made discoveries in algebra and geometry that were not known in Europe until the last century.

In astronomy they ascertained the courses of eclipses, and constructed tables for calculating them, and some of their sages discovered the diurnal revolution of the earth, and calculated its diameter with considerable precision.

All the subtleties of logic and the refinements

of grammar are to be met with in Sanscrit works. In the copious poetic literature of India the niceties and varieties of meter are as numerous as in that of ancient Greece.

It should be remembered that the Hindoos acquired their knowledge by their genius, while the present nations of Europe are largely indebted for theirs to the ancient Greeks and Romans.

The invasion of the country by the Mohammedans crushed the spirit of inquiry and improvement among the people, and the Hindoo mind has for centuries lain dormant. The Mohammedans invaded the land about A.D. 1000. The history of their supremacy is made up largely of war and oppression. Thousands of Hindoos were carried into captivity. During their reign, life, property, and honor were not secure. As a native writer says, "the effect of their government on the country resembled that of a scorching blast upon a plant." Their reign extended until the battle of Plassey, in 1737, from which time British power in the East takes its date.

The English government in India is a great blessing to the people. The Mohammedans would doubtless rejoice if they could regain their former sway, and they have at times laid schemes to that end; but their successive failures have given them the impression that the British power is sustained by God and cannot be overthrown. Some of their most learned moulvais now say that the Christian religion must spread over all the world, consequently the world must be governed by those who will not hinder its progress.

Protestant missions were commenced in 1706, by Schwartz and others, and were encouraged by the King of Denmark, who had previously formed trading settlements in various places in India. Those missionaries, however, failed of achieving great results, by allowing heathen customs to intermingle with the Christian observances of their converts.

The British government for many years made no effort to introduce Christianity, and even forbade missionaries to settle in the country; and when at the close of the eighteenth century Carey, and Thomas, and others of the English Baptists, sought to establish a mission, they were compelled to seek an asylum at the Danish settlement of Serampore, on the banks of the Hooghly, fifteen miles above Calcutta.

"The Marquis of Wellesley gave encouragement to devout missionaries of every Christian persuasion; but during the administrations of Lord Minto and the Marquis of Hastings there was direct opposition to the ministers of the cross, who were obliged to proceed from England to the United States, and sail in an American vessel to their destination. "Some were not permitted to land on British ground, others were obliged to re-embark. Ships were refused port entrance if they had missionaries on board as they were deemed more dangerous than the plague, or the invasion of a French army.

"The governor of Serampore, when desired by the Calcutta authorities to expel Drs. Carey, Marshman, and others, nobly replied, they might compel him to pull down the flag of the Danish king, but he would not refuse a refuge and a home to those whose sole object was the temporal and spiritual welfare of their fellow-beings.

"Despite the most powerful official discountenance, the missionary cause ultimately triumphed. The Church of England became an effective auxiliary. Calcutta in 1814 was made the see of a bishop, under Dr. Middleton; and his amiable successor, Bishop Heber, removed many prejudices, and paved the way for a general recognition of the necessity and duty of affording to the people of India the means of becoming acquainted with the precepts of Christianity.

"The thin edge of the wedge being thus fairly inserted in the stronghold of idolatry, the force of truth drove it home; point by point, step by step, the government was fairly beaten from positions which became untenable.

"It was tardily admitted that some missionaries were good men, and did not intend nor desire to overthrow the dominion of England in the East; next it was acknowledged that they had a direct and immediate interest in upholding the authorities, as the most effectual security for the prosecution of their pious labors. "Soon the government ceased to dismiss civil and military servants because they had become Christians; then came the public avowal of their faith by many of the Europeans in India, and the open celebration of its rites.

"When this vantage ground was gained, other triumphs necessarily followed. "The Scriptures, which the British and Foreign Bible Society, and also the Baptists, had been engaged in translating and printing, were now freely distributed. "Toleration was no longer conceded to Hindooism and other idolatries only: it was extended to Christianity; and the principle was urged boldly that the state should renounce all countenance in the shameful orgies of Juggernaut and other pagan abominations; that the car of this idol and its obscene priests should cease to be annually decorated with scarlet cloth and tinsel, specially provided by the East India Company; and that the troops, English and Mohammedan, should no longer have their feelings outraged by being compelled to do honor to disgusting rites which were a mockery to the true and living God."*

The missionary cause, thus "tolerated," extended and widened from year to year, until in 1862 there were in Hindoostan 519 foreign missionaries, 140 native catechists, and 153,816 native Christians.

There were 70,709 boys and 19,997 girls in mission schools. Since the Mohammedan's lawless reign, the Hindoos of high caste have kept their wives and daughters closely secluded; and this custom, with the Mohammedan plan of keeping their females closely confined in zenanas, forms a very great barrier in obtaining access to women of the higher classes; nevertheless these obstacles are yielding to the persevering efforts of Christians, and the prejudices of the natives in regard to female education are fast vanishing.

Our own mission was commenced in 1856 by Rev. Wm. Butler, who settled in the city of Bareilly, Rohilcund. Our field of labor extends over a good part of the valley north of the Ganges, and embraces the provinces of Oude and Rohilcund, and part of the contiguous sub-Himalayan Range. It is nearly four hundred

* See "British Possessions in Asia," by R. Montgomery Martin, Esq.

miles in length and seventy-five in breadth, with a population of about thirteen millions.

Until our mission was established this part of the country had been entirely neglected, so that we have had to meet the prejudices of the people and the discouragements incident to the work in full force; but God has graciously given us even thus early many tokens of his favor.

In February, 1865, we had 26 native preachers and catechists, 209 native Christians, and 208 orphan children, wholly in our charge. We had 15 stations, 10 chapels, and 1,231 scholars in our mission schools.

The work is now opening in every direction. People of all classes are willing and anxious to be taught *secular* knowledge, and for the sake of this will receive religious instruction. Even the "purdah" is withdrawn to admit female missionaries to the charmed precincts of the zenana.

We can ask no more of them; the rest must be accomplished by the Spirit of God and the faithfulness of the Church. Let the Church then continue to send out the missionaries of Jesus, and not fail to speed their efforts for the salvation of men by her prayers.

It is not a service of ease and luxury, and if any make it such they are unfit for their responsible position. It is a work for which cultivated, earnest, self-denying, consistent, humble, and industrious men and women are needed. There ought to be many such in the Church, willing to devote themselves to this work. Let them be sent forth and heartily and prayerfully sustained.

It is not because of any supposed literary merit in these letters that they have been prepared for publication, but in the hope that they might give some items of information in regard to a people of whom but little is known, but toward whom, at the present time, the attention of the Christian world is directed. If they shall in any degree contribute to increase the interest felt in the missionary work, they will not have been written in vain.

I have not aimed to give in them an historical sketch of our mission, but merely to relate our own every day experience, thinking that I could thus best give a correct idea of our work in India, and if at times they seem dry and uninteresting they are no less matter-of-fact.

Missionaries do not always live on the mountain top, full of hope and enthusiasm; they are often buffeted, depressed, and anxious, like those in the work at home. So also with their work: it is not all prose, but neither is it all poetry; and in order to carry it on successfully, a calm, steadfast reliance upon God is indispensable.

It is a glorious work! It is a blessed privilege to go to the regions beyond, to be pioneers in the work of evangelization; but those that go need to be girt with the "armor of righteousness on the right hand and on the left."

E. J. Humphrey.

CONTENTS.

LETTER I.

LETTER II.

LETTER III.

LETTER IV.

LETTER V.

LETTER VI.

LETTER VII.

LETTER VIII.

LETTER IX.

LETTER X.

LETTER XI.

LETTER XII.

LETTER XIII.

LETTER XIV.

LETTER XV.

LETTER XVI.

LETTER XVII.

LETTER XVIII.

LETTER XIX.

Illustrations.

SIX YEARS IN INDIA.

LETTER I.

Sailing from Boston—Atlantic Ocean—Services on Board Ship—South American Coast off the Cape of Good Hope—Storms—Bay of Bengal—Danger off Sand Heads—Pilot—Terrible News—Natives of India—Hooghly River—Calcutta.

CALCUTTA, Oct. 12, 1587.

MY DEAR MOTHER,—As we are now comfortably settled in Calcutta, I have leisure to write you of our voyage and arrival in India. We sailed from Boston, as you know, on the first day of June, in the good ship Niobe, Captain Storer.

It was a rainy, unpleasant morning, but a large number of people came on board. Dr. Durbin, the corresponding secretary of our Missionary Board, Rev. D. Terry, and Dr. and Mrs. Peck of New York, were also with us.

We met in the ship's cabin, where Dr. Durbin delivered a parting address and commended us to the keeping of God. We then bade our friends good-by, the anchor was weighed, and the Niobe bore us seaward.

Our party consisted of Mr. and Mrs. Pierce and their little babe, Mrs. Owen, of the American Presbyterian Mission in India, and ourselves. We remained on deck gazing upon those lovely and beloved shores till they could no longer be distinguished. "Shall we never see this dear land again?" we involuntarily asked ourselves as the last point disappeared, and we felt ourselves cut adrift from the safe moorings of home and country.

Our gallant ship sped boldly on her course, away, away into the dim distance of angry waters. I forgot all my fears in the sublimity of our surroundings, there was something so solemn, as well as so grand, in the isolation and danger of our position, cut off entirely thus from all human aid.

It soon became necessary for us to arrange our state-rooms, for sundry sensations warned us that a time was fast approaching when exertion would not be practicable.

Our apprehensions were more than realized. For over a week, all our company, except Mrs. Owen, kept mostly to their rooms, and woful sounds and lamentations were often heard. Day after day the ship rolled and pitched about on the heaving sea, a provokingly fine wind giving us little chance to rest.

The latter part of the second week we all began to rally, and as the Sabbath was calm and pleasant, we were able to be present on deck at the service which Captain Storer kindly permitted to be held. The officers, and all the sailors that could be spared from duty, were present. The capstan served for a pulpit as well as an anchor for the speaker, and seats were spirited up from parts unknown to us, and ranged around it for the little congregation. The precious words of divine truth, the singing, the prayers, all sounded very sweetly to our ears, mingled as they were with the low murmurings of the Atlantic waters.

We had morning and evening prayers regularly throughout the voyage, and a Bible-class every Thursday evening. Many a time when we knelt we were obliged to cling to the stationary sofas by the dining-table to keep our balance, on account of the rolling of the vessel; but this did not prevent our enjoying the precious privilege of prayer.

We had a very uneventful voyage down the Atlantic, but the novelty of sea-life kept us from being lonely. Toward the last of June the winds bore us too much in a westerly direction, and on the fourth of July we found ourselves in the vicinity of the South American coast, near Cape St. Roque. The main land could be only faintly discerned with the aid of a telescope, but an island was plainly visible all day. It was the Fernando Noronha Island, used by the Brazilian government as a place of banishment for convicts.

The easterly winds and the lee shore were not very pleasant; but after a great deal of "tacking ship" we succeeded in getting further out to sea. We were detained in the torrid zone for a number of days by light variable winds and calms, and suffered extremely from the intense heat. The calm weather continued for some time, and we were only able to make about seventy-five miles daily until we crossed the tropic of Capricorn and entered the south temperate zone. The wind then increased until it culminated in a grand gale, broken by occasional squalls of hail. The waves ran mountain high, and when bursting in the sunshine, threw out innumerable rainbows of brightest hues.

As we were approaching the Cape of Good Hope in the winter season (the seasons are inverted south of the equator you know) we had reason to expect very severe storms. Sea-pigeons, cape-hens, and occasionally a beautiful albatross, came circling round our ship, and the sailors had much amusement in catching them. The albatross is a very large bird. Some of those we caught, when both wings were extended, measured over three yards across.

Off the Cape the weather was very cold; but

we had no storms except squalls of wind and hail. We saw the phosphorus in the water in the vicinity of the Cape. For several nights the ship seemed to be sailing on a sea of fire, and her wake a track of brilliant sparks.

On the eleventh of August a brisk west wind carried us quite out of the neighborhood of the Cape, and increased to such a gale as we had not previously experienced.

For nine days the wind blew with terrific violence. Our ship was "hove to" several times, heavy waves broke over her and came into the cabin in showers. We had great difficulty in getting our meals, on account of the violent pitching of the vessel, which made it almost an impossibility to move about at all. During the remainder of our voyage we were continually threatened with storms, but were really overtaken by nothing worse than violent squalls.

We reached the light-ship off Sandhead September 17, and fully expected to receive a pilot on board then and there. We came up alongside the vessel at ten o'clock P. M., and were received, according to usage, with a splendid blue light, and a rocket; but no pilot came on board, and we were obliged to cast anchor and wait quietly till morning to ascertain the reason why.

The morning brought great anxiety. There

was no pilot-brig in sight, nothing but the solitary light-ship. She was very tardy in answering our signals, but finally told us that the pilot-brig usually there had been driven ashore in a recent storm, and we must go to another point for a pilot. The question then was, "What is to be done?" We had consumed the greater part of the day in obtaining the intelligence that we must look elsewhere for a pilot. We were anchored in an exceeding dangerous position, being very near some invisible sandbanks, and exposed to the force of the currents which set in toward the land in the morning, and changing about mid-day, set strongly seaward. The other light-ship was about five hours' sail from us with the light wind we then had. The turbid, angry waters lashed the sides of our good ship with a mournful sound, and the clouds betokened an approaching storm.

All our sails were furled, and two of our anchors imbedded in the sand. The captain decided to weigh the anchor, and gave the necessary orders. He appeared extremely anxious. The oldest sailor on board was placed at the helm, and others were directed to stand ready by the ropes in order to unfurl the upper sails the moment the order should be given. If the sails had been unfurled too soon, we might have lost our anchors; but if, on the contrary, they had not been spread soon enough, the current would have sent us aground, and our gallant Niobe, which had borne us safely over so many thousands of trackless miles, would have capsized, and probably every soul of us would have been lost.

The anchors were weighed, and rapidly as possible the sails were being unfurled. We stood in breathless suspense on the deck, the missionaries were hard at work with the sailors, when the captain, who stood bareheaded in the hot sun, watching every motion of the sailors and the ship, while heavy perspiration poured off his face, exclaimed in a frenzied manner, as he saw we were being drawn near a sandbank, "My God, we are lost!" It was a terrible moment; but almost immediately another sail was set, and the ship righted on her course toward the other light-ship.

At nine o'clock that evening Captain S. came down into the cabin where we were all sitting, and said smilingly, "My good friends, I am happy to inform you that we have reached the light-ship." We hastened on deck and beheld a delightful sight indeed. Not merely one, but a dozen or more ships were about us. We felt restored to the world of mankind again, and rejoiced that our long solitary voyage was indeed over. Alas, we little knew what terrible tidings would reach us on the morrow!

The morning of the nineteenth of September dawned clear and lovely. The threatening storm had passed over. About eight o'clock a boat put off from one of the ships and came alongside with a pilot. "There," said Captain Storer to us, "there are some of the people you have come to benefit." We looked over the bulwarks with intense interest to obtain our first sight of the natives of Hindoostan. There they were, six small well-formed men, with shining brown skins, straight black hair, and regular, pleasant features. They were bare-headed, and wore ever so little clothing, merely a strip of cloth wound about their loins. The pilot, although well dressed, looked nearly as dark as they, and Captain S. remarked that he was evidently of mixed descent. He came on board at once, and upon Captain Storer's invitation followed us down into the cabin, bringing with him a bundle of newspapers.

"You have heard the news, I suppose," he asked. "I don't know why you should suppose so," said Captain S. "We left the port of Boston June 1, and have not made land since, nor spoken a vessel for over two months."

The pilot looked round upon us as if to note the effect of his words as he said, "Well, the Sepoy army has mutinied throughout all Northern India, the people have generally assisted them, and they have massacred most of the European residents in the different stations."

Mrs. Owen, whose husband had remained at his work while she made the home visit, sank into a seat in great agitation. "Are the missionaries at Allahabad murdered?" she asked. "No," said he, "I think not; some of them I know are in Calcutta, and perhaps all; I am not certain on that point."

Then it was our turn. "What about Bareilly?" we asked with sinking hearts.

"There were several murdered there," he answered; "but most of the residents escaped to Nynee Tal, a station in the Sub-Himalayas, about seventy-five miles from Bareilly, where they are comparatively safe, as the hill-men have not mutinied, and the nawab of Rampore, a small native state, which lies between the two places, is loyal to the government." He gave us the newspapers, saying we would learn from them all we wished, and much more, and then he went on deck to his duties.

What a sudden crushing of all our hopes and plans was this terrible intelligence! We looked at each other in blank silence when we were left alone, half paralyzed by the shock we had received. Not until we had talked the matter over, and read some of the newspaper accounts, could we realize the extent of the calamity that had befallen us.

Befallen *us* indeed! Why, what reason we had for gratitude to God that calms and contrary winds had hindered our earlier arrival. But the European residents of India, how our hearts ached for them as we read of the successive outbreaks and massacres at Meerut, Delhi, Bareilly, Shahjehanpore, Allahabad, Futteghur, and the horrible butchery at Cawnpore! Our tears fell fast as we read of the devoted band of missionaries from our own land who were martyred there. Of four families but one child escaped. He was the son of Mr. Campbell, and being an invalid had been sent to a hill station in the care of a chaplain of the Church of England.

What indignities they suffered, what agonies they endured, no one knows; nothing further than that, having left their home in Futteghur in company with the surviving residents, they came down in boats near Cawnpore, where they were captured by a party of troopers belonging to the infamous Nana Sahib, and taken to Cawnpore, where they were shot a few hours after their arrival.

The lists of murdered and escaped residents of Bareilly were given; but as Mr. Butler's name was omitted in both lists, we were left in uncertainty regarding his fate until we reached Calcutta. That place also had been in great danger, and but two weeks previous to our arrival indications of an outbreak were so marked that the frightened residents took refuge on board the shipping. It was safe at this time, however, as the citizens had armed and organized themselves into a military corps, and the Sepoy regiments (that is, native soldiery) had been disarmed.

We anchored off Saugur Island, just at the entrance of the Hoogley river, the night after taking the pilot on board. The next morning, which was the Sabbath, dawned brightly upon scenes strange to us. The land lay on either side of us, flat and marshy; south was the open sea, north the turbid river.

A boat full of natives came alongside early in the day, and after considerable bargaining, remained to help work the ship, as the frequent casting of the lead, changing of the sails, weighing and casting anchors, etc., was very fatiguing. These boatmen are called "lascars." They fastened their boat to the stern of our ship, and prepared and ate their food on it, so that their caste should not be injured by too close contact with "Feringhees," as they call white foreigners.

Their curry, which we watched them prepare over a little fire built on an iron plate, was composed of fish cut up in pieces and cooked with a finely powdered mixture of spices, garlic, and onions, with sufficient oil to make a rich gravy! Captain S. had some prepared for the table, but it was so hot with cayenne pepper that we could not eat it.

We passed up the river some distance that day, and anchored just above the bar James and Mary. We thought the scenery very tame and dreary, although the "feathery palm trees" rose thickly in occasional groves, and little villages, or collections of mud and straw huts, dotted the fields. Several kinds of fruit were brought on board during the day. We liked the bananas better than any other kind we tasted.

With the morning tide we recommenced our course up the river. We saw some singular looking objects floating past our ship at different points during the day, and upon inquiry learned that they were corpses! Had we not a strangely disagreeable reception in India? First, tidings of the cruelty of the people, and second, these silent loathsome witnesses of their superstition! We learned from Mrs. Owen, that away from the sea in the inland portion of the country, the Hindoos burn their deceased friends, and scatter their bones and ashes on the Ganges, of which the Hooghly is a branch, but near the sea they sometimes cast them in without burning.

We anchored at evening, September 21st, opposite the ex-king of Oude's palace, near our proper moorings in the port of Calcutta.

The tide turned too early for us to reach our

An Indian River.

proper position, as we had expected; but we were, after all, but a short distance down the stream.

You are aware that we had letters of introduction to Messrs. Stewart and Young, of Calcutta. We were doubly glad that was the case when we learned the state of the country, and were especially grateful to Mr. Young for hastening on board that evening to relieve our anxiety. To our great joy and relief we learned that Mr. Butler and family were safe in Nynee Tal. By his directions Mr. Young has rented and furnished a house for us in Calcutta, as we cannot possibly go to our mission field now, and probably will not be able to for a long time to come.

The last night we spent on the Niobe was very trying. The heat was almost stifling, the musquitoes almost maddening, and the incessant shrieks and mournful cries of the jackals almost terrifying! What fancy could have taken Bishop Heber, who wrote so many sensible things, that he should ever say so absurd a thing as the "Jackal's sylvan notes?"

The morning of the 22d was necessarily a busy time, as we expected to land quite early. While in the midst of our labors a tall gentleman rushed down the stairs and inquired for Mrs. Owen. It was her husband, and you may imagine her joy at seeing him safe and well.

Messrs. Stewart and Young came for us about two o'clock P.M. We were not sorry to leave the Niobe. Nearly four months of sea life had thoroughly wearied us of its sameness, and yet as we thought of the state of the country and the uncertainty of our prospects, the ship seemed like a refuge to which we might be glad to return, where we should have only the elements to battle with.

We were assisted into a native boat, called a dinghy, and were soon rowed ashore, where we found two cabs in waiting, and we were soon set down at the residence of our good friends Messrs. Stewart and Young.

As there are so many things that strike us as strange all about us, I will defer all descriptions till my next.

LETTER II.

First Impressions of Calcutta—First Dinner on Shore—Native Servants, Punkahs—Curry—Housekeeping—Studying the Language—A Native Christian—Dr. Duff—Mr. Poorie—Palanquins—Buksheesh—The Mutiny—The Climate.

CALCUTTA, Nov. 1, 1857.

MY DEAR MOTHER,—In order to give you something of an idea of the strangeness of everything that met our eyes upon our arrival, I will commence my descriptions at Garden Reach, the landing place, where we took carriages.

As we drove through the suburbs and streets of the city we were astonished at the swarming population. The shops were open to the streets, and full of half naked men and boys. The streets, also, were teeming with life, and from the mud and straw huts came the sound of many voices. We came to the European residences, and although they did not quite meet our expectations of the "City of Palaces," they certainly were lofty and airy-looking dwellings.

We soon arrived at the house of our friends; for although Mr. Stewart's family is in Scotland and Mr. Young is unmarried, they yet keep house. We were at once shown up a wide staircase, as they and most Europeans use the first floor only for storage, offices, etc., on account of its dampness.

At four o'clock we were summoned to dinner, and were gratified with the evidence it afforded us that Mohammedan cooks can prepare extremely palatable dishes. The servants are very different from the boatmen and common people of the streets in dress and manners. The table servants dress with great neatness in long loose white cotton trousers, long half-fitting coats, and white muslin turbans. The custom in Calcutta is to have a waiter or khidmatgar for each member of a family, a khansąmah, or steward, to oversee everything relating to the table, and a cook, or vawurchee. This latter individual never appears to public view, but leads a retired life among the pots and kettles of the cookhouse.

The Hindoos cannot become our cooks or table servants, as their religion forbids their touching meat. They pull the punkahs, keep the house in order, run on errands, and are durbans, or gatekeepers. Their dress is composed of a smaller turban than the Mohammedan sports, or else a small white cotton cap called a topee, a short coat which opens on the right side, in contradistinction to the Mohammedans, which opens on the left, and a long piece of copperas-colored cotton folded about the loins in such a manner as to form long lappets falling down to their knees. This cloth is the only part of their attire which they wear while taking their food, as every other article of their apparel has been rendered unclean by having been in the hands of men of a lower caste to be washed; but this article is washed daily by themselves, and so kept holy!

But I must not fail to describe the punkahs. They form too important an accessory to our comfort to be forgotten. There is first a frame of wood about twelve feet in length and one foot in width, which is covered smoothly with coarse cloth, which is afterward painted, and ornamented so cleverly as to look quite like wood. This is suspended from the ceiling by ropes, just low enough to allow people to pass under after a heavy double frill, about ten inches in width, has been attached. In the center is a ring of iron, to which is fastened a rope. This passes through an aperture in the wall left for that purpose, and is pulled steadily by a servant sitting in the hall or verandah. The air of the room is thus kept continually in motion by the punkah, and a certain degree of coolness is obtained.

The European residents do not generally have the punkahs swinging at night, as a fresh sea-breeze makes the nights in Calcutta far more tolerable than the days.

But to return to our dinner at Mr. Stewart's. It was very like an ordinary dinner at home, with the addition of ale and wine. The meats and vegetables were served on double plates filled with hot water. This is necessary on account of the punkah, which cools the food too much if these plates are not used. The second course consisted of rice and curry. The rice was beautifully cooked, every kernel distinct and dry, though perfectly tender. The curry was dressed with clarified butter, called "ghee," instead of oil, and looked very inviting. As our friends assured us we would like it, we attempted to eat a little; but the pungent taste made us glad to relinquish the undertaking.

After dinner, and an early cup of delicious Assam tea, we drove over to our own house. We found it to be similar to Mr. Stewart's in most respects. The one great necessity—coolness—makes much variety in architecture impossible.

There seems to be but one material used for buildings, namely, brick, and the walls are always plastered on both sides. The floors and roofs are also of brick and mortar, the latter being made over wooden beams. The rooms are high, varying from sixteen to twenty-five feet, and are all large, and abundantly supplied with glass folding-doors instead of windows. There are also green blinds, which quite exclude the intense glare of the sun. At night we fasten the blinds and open the glass doors to admit the air. The floors are covered with a fine matting.

The trials of housekeeping under such unusual circumstances were much lightened by the kindness of our friends. They gave us for our khansamah one of their own servants, on account of his being able to speak a little broken English. We would find it a difficult matter to get on comfortably without him, as we cannot well always have a dictionary at hand. This language looks like a great mountain; shall we ever scale it? We are studying almost constantly now, as we have the long-coveted helps. We use Forbes's Grammar, and have Forbes's, Shakspeare's, and Yates's dictionaries.

Our teacher or moonshee is John Caleb, a native Christian catechist, who belongs to the American Presbyterian Mission in Allahabad. He was educated in that mission from a child, and was so well known for his earnest piety that when the mutiny occurred in Allahabad, and the Sepoys did not succeed in finding him, they offered a reward of five hundred rupees ($250) for his head. When Mr. Owen came to Calcutta he brought Caleb with him. We have engaged his services as moonshee, and he occupies a room in our house. He speaks English very well.

Although we have been but a few days over

a month in Calcutta we have made quite a large number of acquaintances.

We were invited to tea by the Rev. Dr. Duff soon after our arrival, and passed a delightful evening at his house.

Dr. Duff is a veteran in the missionary service. He is at the head of the educational department, and has a college for native youth in charge, which is said to be a very fine institution. He is from the land of Bruce, and is a fine scholar, a very eloquent preacher, and an earnest and devoted missionary. He is very genial in his manners, and gives one an exalted idea of Scotchmen in general. We were also invited a few evenings since to the house of the Rev. Mr. Poorie, where we met Mr. and Mrs. Owen, and quite a large company of Calcutta missionaries.

Mr. and Mrs. Poorie are in charge of an orphanage for native girls, which now has fifty inmates. Mrs. P. superintends the establishment mostly, and has several classes in the school. Mr. P. is associated with Dr. Duff in the college.

Instead of always calling a garee or cab when we wish to go out, we occasionally use the palkees, or palanquins, as the Europeans call them. They are very like the pictures we have seen of them. A palkee is made of nicely painted wood, shaped like a trunk, long enough to lie down in, high enough to sit in, comfortably cushioned, with sliding-doors at the sides. Two short poles are firmly fastened at each end near the top, by which natives carry the vehicle on their shoulders. There are feet at each corner which prevent it from being quite level with the ground when set down. It is usually only large enough for one person.

Four men, two at each end, carry it, and if the distance is great, two or four men go along to change. These men are Hindoos, of the caste called kahars. A number of them club together, buy a palkee, and carry people for their living. There is rarely any difficulty in calling one when we wish to go out.

There is one objection to them, and that is the fact that when you lie down in one you cannot be certain that your predecessor was the kind of person you would like to follow. Perhaps it was a drunken soldier or a half-crazed sailor, (Calcutta is thronged with them,) perhaps an oily Hindoo gentleman, a "baboo," as he is called; anybody who possessed money enough to pay the fare.

The kahars are never satisfied with the usual fare, but always clamor for a gratuity, "buksheesh," as they term it. You were either very heavy, and they had a hard time of it, or you were so thin and feeble looking that they carried you with extraordinary care. For some plausible reason or other you certainly ought to give them buksheesh. They travel with a sort of half-trotting step, accompanying each motion with a shrug of the shoulders and a lugubrious "ugh."

It is said that they often indulge in remarks to each other not at all complimentary to the occupant of the palkee, such as, "He is a heavy fellow, my brother; let's throw him down;" and another will answer, "O but he has a terrible temper, he will beat us," etc.

The country remains in much the same state as when we landed; but when the troops that have recently arrived shall reach the upper provinces the mutiny will probably be put down immediately. Generals Neal and Havelock, with their small band, forced their way into Lucknow to the relief of the beleaguered garrison, but they are still too few to free the place. General Neal was killed when they were entering the city. A mine was found by the relieving party which would probably have destroyed the fortifications if it had not been thus fortunately discovered.

The weather is very oppressive, hot and close. The rainy season is considered closed, although we have occasional showers.

The houses are much discolored by the long rains, and in many places are covered with fine green moss. Little shrubs have sprung up on the roofs and in crevices of the walls. The atmosphere is stormy and malarious. Cholera is said to be very prevalent, but not unusually so for this season of the year. Europeans do not seem to be very much afraid of its ravages, I suppose because they are so accustomed to its presence, as there is more or less of it in the city all the year round.

LETTER III.

Calcutta — Its Early History — Public Buildings — Botanical Gardens — New Year — An Ayah — Mr. Lacroix — Visit at Examination of a Native School — State of the Country — Preparations to leave Calcutta.

CALCUTTA, *February* 20, 1858.

MY DEAR MOTHER,—While war, with all its attendant horrors, has been ravaging the land, we have dwelt securely in this city, and been busily preparing ourselves for our future work by studying the language and, so far as we can, the manners and customs of the people.

Calcutta is situated on the east bank of the Hooghly River, about one hundred miles from its mouth. It was a small village when acquired by the English in 1700, in the center of which stood an old black building called by the natives "kalee kotee," that is, black house, hence the anglicized name Calcutta.

Beyond the Mahratta Ditch (an intrenchment intended as a defense against the incursions of the Mahratta tribe) are the suburbs of Chitpore, Bhowaneepore, Alipore, and others. On the opposite side of the river are the villages of Seebpore, Howrah, and Sulkeah. The city is defended by Fort William, which is built of an octagonal form, and mounts six hundred and nineteen guns. Among the public buildings are the Government House and the Town Hall, both fine structures, the Mohammedan and Hindoo colleges, Metcalfe Hall, and the Ochterlony Monument.

About three miles below the city, on the Howrah side of the river, there are extensive botanical gardens, laid out with good taste and effect.

The most elevated part of Calcutta is only thirty feet above the sea level. It is thought probable that some day the city may be wholly submerged. In May, 1850, the population of Calcutta, exclusive of suburbs, was 413,182.

We visited the botanical gardens on Christmas Day and saw many brilliant flowers and magnificent trees. Messrs. Stewart and Young, also Mr. and Mrs. Owen, accompanied us. Our khansamah carried a basket of refreshments, and arranged them very nicely on a table-cloth spread on the grass.

We sat around on shawls, quite in oriental fashion. The Banian tree was the most remarkable object we saw. It covers an area of about half an acre. The ground under it is paved, and seats are placed at convenient distances.

Another very great attraction to foreigners is a beautiful scarlet-leaved tree, which is about as high as our own Mountain Ash. The leaves are long and grow in clusters, in the centers of which are several tiny pale green buds. There is not a green leaf on the tree, and the effect of the sunlight upon the red leaves is most gorgeous.

On New Year's eve we dined with our gentlemen friends. Our thoughts often turned homeward, and I presume theirs did also; but we nevertheless passed a very pleasant evening.

We recently attended a very interesting examination of the Mission School of the London Missionary Society at Bhowaneepore. It is at present in the charge of Rev. E. Storrow. There are more than four hundred lads in attendance. Essays were read upon the necessity and obligation of maintaining family prayer, and similar subjects, by nominal Hindoos. To all appearance they were thorough believers in the Christian religion, and probably it is so; but the strong bond of caste keeps them within the pale of Hindooism. The Asiatic Museum, which we have visited twice, contains a fine collection of works of nature and art.

We occasionally drive out on the "strand," which is a broad road on the bank of the Hooghly, and is a place of general resort every evening. Hundreds of carriages, drawn by spirited horses, with gayly-dressed natives in attendance, together with humbler equipages, and ladies and gentlemen on horseback, throng the street. Often a party of sailors, intent on making the most of their stay in port, hire a couple of ponies, and, with two or three on each, mingle in the crowd.

I have not yet told you of our female servant. She is an ayah, or nurse for Mrs. Pierce's babe, and is a very agreeable addition to our household. With her came our first knowledge of native women, except so far as we could judge by the Bengalee women of low caste whom we see in the streets. She is a Mussulmanee, as the female followers of Mohammed are called. She wears muslin trowsers, and over them a long skirt of the same material, and a short loose jacket with short sleeves, which leave her arms free to be decorated with bracelets. She always has her head, shoulders, and waist enveloped in a chuddur, which is a piece of muslin about three yards in length and one and a half in width. She puts this over her head, and crossing her chest, throws one end of it gracefully over one shoulder. She wears bracelets, earrings, finger and toe rings, of silver.

The missionaries of different denominations are very much united here. Every month they meet on an appointed morning and breakfast together, after which they discuss the interests of the missionary work, read essays, hold discussions, etc. Mr. Lacroix stands at the head of the preaching department. He is a native of Switzerland, but is in the employ of the London Missionary Society. He has been over thirty years in India engaged in the missionary work. His head is now sprinkled with silver, but his form is erect, and his face beams with kindly feeling. He is a noble man, and a most laborious missionary. He is said to be remarkably proficient in the Bengalee language, as is also his eldest daughter, Mrs. Mullens. Dr. and Mrs. Mullens are also engaged in the missionary work.

We have spent several delightful evenings at Mr. Lacroix's home, in the society of his charming family and invited guests, and our memories of those occasions will always be pleasant. We feel very grateful indeed to all the missionaries and other Christian friends in Calcutta for the kind courtesies and sympathy they have extended toward us.

Caleb has returned to Allahabad, but he remained long enough with us to render very valuable aid in commencing our studies. We held religious services every Sabbath morning while he remained with us. Our servants, at our request, were always present, and the missionaries preached to them in turn, with Caleb as interpreter. All behaved very well, except the cook. We were quite astonished indeed to find we had so zealous a Mussulman in our cookhouse. He often interrupted Caleb, saying, "Jesus is not the Son of God, he is only a prophet, and not so great a prophet as Mohammed either." Caleb always answered him with admirable patience.

The missionaries have also had many opportunities to preach in English in various parts of the city, owing to the frequent vacancies caused by sickness, absence, etc.

For several weeks past we have had social meetings in our parlor on Wednesday evenings. Mr. Stewart and two other gentlemen of our acquaintance, who are Wesleyans, meet with us. A Wesleyan soldier who landed one Wednesday, and had but one evening to spend in Calcutta, inquired for a Wesleyan prayer-meeting, and was directed to our house. He came in and seemed to enjoy meeting with us exceedingly.

Our stay in Calcutta is fast drawing to a termination. We expect to leave in a few days. Whether we shall succeed in joining Mr. Butler, who has come down to Meerut, is somewhat doubtful; but it seems best to try. If we succeed we shall go to Nynee Tal, and remain until the country is sufficiently settled for us to commence our work on the plains. It would be very desirable for us to be in Nynee Tal during the ensuing hot season, as the mountain climate is delightful. The prospect of peace is brighter because the war is waged more vigorously.

A large number of women and children from Lucknow, with the remains of the worn-out garrison who held out so long against fearful odds, have safely arrived in Allahabad, and will soon arrive in Calcutta. They were got away by a very clever stratagem of Sir Colin Campbell's, too late, however, to save the brave and good Havelock, who had been ill for some time. He was brought away in a dying state, and lies buried a short distance from Lucknow, toward Cawnpore. It yet remains to conquer the immense native army still in possession of Lucknow, and to retake Rohilcund.

Another battle at Lucknow is imminent.

If we go further up the country than Benares we must go quickly, as immediately upon the dispersion of the army at Lucknow the country will be overrun by marauders.

Delhi, Meerut, Agra, Cawnpore, and Allahabad are quietly in possession of English troops. Benares is considered so safe that people are permitted to go there from Calcutta if they can; but as the steamers, horses, and kahars are all monopolized by government to transport troops and stores up the country, it is not an easy matter for civilians to travel. We are to go in private carriages drawn by kahars. We know it is extremely doubtful about always finding enough of them unemployed to take us along, but there certainly is no other way. Mr. Pierce's family will travel in a phaeton, and we have engaged what is called a palkee-garee, belonging to a gentleman in Allahabad, who is agent for a horse dak, that is, staging company. He is to give us passage by horse dak from Allahabad to Meerut if we take his garee safely to the former place. Mr. Parry, an old resident in the country, is to take charge of the expedition, as he speaks the language fluently and understands the native character. He and his family have but recently escaped from Lucknow.

We were at a loss to know what to do with our house, which was rented for a year; but that, with all our furniture, was taken off our hands by the Relief Committee, and some of the tired refugees from Lucknow will soon find shelter here.

But one more problem remained unsolved: how could our baggage be conveyed up the country? The missionaries resolved to make one more attempt to procure a passage for it by the steamers, and this time they were successful. They interested one of the captains in our enterprise, and he agreed to send our boxes up to Benares by the three next steamers, four boxes to go by each. Thus the last obstacles have vanished, and in so signal a manner as to leave no doubt in our minds in regard to our duty. So we go forth in the name of the Lord, not knowing what may befall us. We see our way clear to Benares. A friend there has invited us to his house, where we can remain until our way shall open to go on. Do not be anxious about us. Whatever may come, we are sure that we go forth under the direction and with the blessing of God, and you know we are not our own, to do our own will and pleasure, but we are bought with a price, even the precious blood of Jesus. We would "own him Lord, and in his footsteps tread."

We are none of us in robust health. I have had the severest illness this season that I ever had, and am still far from well. I think it possible the journey may do me good. We have so arranged our carriages that we can sleep quite comfortably, and thus we can travel night and day without great weariness.

We have made several shopping excursions to look up hot water plates and other things in which we find ourselves deficient. We visited the old and new China bazars in our search. The shopkeepers are not all Chinamen, as the name would seem to imply; but there are many who, with the Hindoostanee merchants, quite bewildered us with their jargon. The bazars are crowded constantly, and the tumult is something overwhelming. The shopkeepers spy new-comers very quickly, and with every imaginable piece of merchandise in hand they crowd around, shouting in broken English, "Buy this box, mem sahib? Very fine picture! you buy?" "Here is lovely bonnet, mem sahib." "What else you buy, mem sahib? See, very fine book, magnificent combs, mem sahib," etc., etc. We could scarcely endure the noise long enough to buy what we wanted, and were glad to leave the busy scene.

The hot season is fast approaching, and we are told that punkahs will be swinging again in two weeks. But we shall find it as cool in Meerut the last of March as now in Calcutta, so we hope the heat will not be overpowering during any portion of our journey.

LETTER IV.

Leaving Calcutta—Mr. Parry—Manner of Traveling—Vindhya Hills—Hindoo Legend concerning them—Progress up the Country—Impressions of Benares—Mr. Heinig.

BENARES, March 6, 1858.

MY DEAR MOTHER,—We left Calcutta on the 24th of last month, crossed the Hooghly, and took the cars at Howrah for Raneegunge. We slept on the floor of the station house at Raneegunge, about one hundred and twelve miles from Calcutta, the night of the 24th.

The next morning our carriages, which had been sent up by rail the day previous, were drawn up by the station house, and our baggage arranged. Ours was a small garee with two seats opposite each other, like a cab.

Our most valuable luggage was first placed in the space between the seats, and over it some small boxes of provision; then two boards were fitted over the place, even with the seats, and our mattress placed over the whole, with blankets and pillows. Our trunks occupied the top of the garee. Mr. Parry called some kahars, and engaged a sufficient number to draw our carriages one stage, about ten miles. One man was sent ahead to gather the same number at the next chowkee or changing place. In this way we traveled both day and night, merely stopping an hour morning and evening to prepare food.

We sometimes stopped at the small houses called dak bungalows, erected by government for the accommodation of travelers; but these were so often found half destroyed that we placed no dependence upon them, but prepared and ate our simple meals under the beautiful mango and tamarind trees that stand near the road.

But I have not told you of the road, and it truly deserves mention; for of all the roads I ever saw, natural, macadamized, plank, or corduroy, the Grand Trunk Road, extending from Calcutta to Peshawur, a distance of eighteen hundred miles, is certainly the best. It is broad, smooth, and hard, being covered with a "calcareous concretion" called kunkur, and beaten down very thoroughly.

The country appears so flat, sandy, and barren, that it would have seemed inconceivably desolate to us, but for the beautiful groves of mango and tamarind trees that dot the fields.

The little villages, with their mud huts and thatched roofs, looked very dirty and poor. The villagers, however, seemed contented, and *easily* industrious, and were invariably respectful and obliging.

On the fourth day we crossed the Vindhya Hills. The Hindoos have a curious legend in regard to their origin.

They say the Rajah of Ceylon stole Seeta, the wife of Ram, one of their gods. Ram at once summoned Hanooman, the king of apes, to his relief. He sent an army of apes, who came flying (!) from the Himalaya Mountains, laden with large stones, to construct a bridge from the continent to Ceylon, so that Ram might be enabled to go over and recover his lost bride. They went back and forth several times for supplies; but finally, as they came flying along fully laden, word came from Raur that the bridge was complete, so they dropped their burdens by the way, which formed this chain of hills.

The Sabbath found us at a small place called Shergotty. We found there a good dak bungalow, and resolved to stay in it through the day, although we knew we were running some risk in doing so, as bands of rebels from various directions were hurrying toward Lucknow, and by remaining long in one place we were, of course, in more danger than when we were traveling.

Toward night some English officers came to the bungalow, and a body of soldiers encamped near it. We were glad to see them, and wished we might have their company all the way to Meerut. Their coming, however, necessitated our departure, and as the evening shades gathered we lay down in our carriage-beds, and proceeded on our journey.

We had heard rumors during the day that Sepoys were lurking about in that part of the country, and we were therefore a little more fearful than usual.

Throughout the night we often fancied we saw stalwart forms starting out from the dim groves, and that we heard strange voices shouting in the distance. But the morning dawned, and we were still unharmed. God had taken care of us.

We crossed the river Soane toward morning. During and immediately after the rains it is a wide stream; in the month of February it is but a rivulet, and so continues until the ensuing rainy season. The bed of the river, however, was no trifle. We were obliged to have an extra number of men to drag our carriages through the deep sand.

Early on Tuesday morning we approached the so-called holy city of Benares. But first was the Ganges, that stream of fearful memories, whose waters are supposed by the deluded Hindoos to be efficacious in cleaning the soul from sin. It was our first view of the "sacred Ganges," and it did not strike us favorably. Although broad, the river is a sluggish, muddy stream, with an appearance strongly suggestive of alligators and Hindoo ashes! Our kahars shouted and gesticulated to make way for us as we crossed the river on the long shaky bridge of boats. The bridge is a rude affair; but as it is often carried away by the rise of the river in the rainy season, I suppose it would not pay to have it look finer.

The native part of the city, through which we passed, looked decidedly Hindooish, much more so than does Calcutta. Calcutta is more anglicized than I realized when there. When I saw the numerous temples of Benares, the ghauts, and frequent groups of fakeers or devotees, I realized that we were just beginning to see heathenism in its real hideousness.

We went directly to the house of Mr. Hienig, a Baptist missionary, now living quite alone in his large bungalow, his wife having gone to England with their children. We met her in Calcutta just before she sailed, and through her kindness received the invitation from Mr. Hienig to occupy rooms in his house while we should wish to stay in Benares.

Immediately upon our arrival we were shown to some pleasant rooms, and told that Mr. Hienig's servants would procure us anything we might require. After breakfast we unpacked fresh clothing and bedding, and gave our soiled clothing over to the tender mercies of a Benares dhobee or washerman. After bathing and dressing, we enjoyed ourselves in looking about the premises. O how delightful it seemed to be safe and quiet once more!

Mr. Hienig's house is a bungalow one story high, on a very low foundation. The roof is thatched with straw, put on a light framework of bamboos in four compartments running up to a point. This kind of roof gives a building a very singular appearance, but it is said to be the coolest kind that can be used in India. The only objections to it are its inflammable nature, and the necessity of renewal every three or four years. The floors and walls are of brick and mortar, as in Calcutta, but not so neatly finished. Overhead cotton cloth is closely fastened in each room, and then whitewashed. These ceilings are called chuts. They look very well, but when the wind blows wave considerably.

There were a great many lizards about the house, which annoyed us somewhat. They fell on the beds and tables, and sometimes on us; but as they are perfectly harmless we were not alarmed, although it was unpleasant to have them make so free.

We enjoyed our visit with Mr. Hienig, and were much interested in his accounts of missionary work.

Benares is situated on the east bank of the Ganges. It is three miles long and about one mile in width. The streets are narrow and crooked. The houses are generally built of sun-dried brick thatched with straw.

Access is gained to the river by ghauts, built at convenient intervals along the banks. "But what are ghauts?" you ask. They are small buildings, something like a pavilion, and are built as near the water as possible. Under them are stairs that go down into the water. The whole affair is built in the most substantial manner, with arches and pillars highly ornamented. In the morning these ghauts are thronged by devout Hindoos as they go down into the sacred waters to bathe.

Benares is a celebrated place of pilgrimage, as its numerous temples and pundits, that is, learned brahmins, render the place very holy in the estimation of the people.

We are to leave to-morrow for Allahabad, thence to Meerut, from which place (if it please God to take us safely there) I will write you.

LETTER V.

Departure from Benares—Arrival at Allahabad—Separation there—Our Visit with Mr. Munnis and Family—Indian Railway—Traveling by Horse Dak—Cawnpore—Agra—Taj-Mahal—Fort—Journey to Meerut.

MEERUT, March 20, 1858.

MY DEAR MOTHER,—Friday morning we left Benares, and Saturday morning, thoroughly wearied, arrived in Allahabad. The heat had increased considerably during our stay in Benares, and traveling became more exhausting every day.

Allahabad (City of God) is situated at the confluence of the Ganges, here one and a half miles in width, and the Jumna, three fourths of a mile in width. The fort, on the east and south, rises directly from the water, and is of great size and strength. The city extends along the Jumna to the west of the fort.

Notwithstanding its advantageous position, it is an ill-built, wretched looking place. It has a population of about seventy thousand. The only building worthy of note is the Jumna Musjed.

We crossed another long villainous bridge of boats, that creaked and swayed as if it greatly wished to let us through, passed some barracks, and then by dint of inquiry went through the city to the premises of the missionaries of the American Presbyterian Board. There we found Mr. and Mrs. Munnis, whose acquaintance we had formed in Calcutta.

Mr. H. took the garee over to its owner, and received the promise of a "horse dak" to Agra, to be ready for us at Caugor, which was then the terminus of the strip of railway just got into operation from Allahabad. Messrs. Pierce and Parry, with their families, went on the same day, as waiting only increased the danger.

As for us, we had no choice; we must wait till Monday. So they went on weary as they were, but we remained and rested. Without that rest I think I could not have lived to reach Meerut. The heat, dust, weariness, irregular meals, and constant uneasiness, had brought on a low nervous fever, which reduced me greatly. Sunday I was better, although still suffering.

We went in the evening to an English service in the mission chapel, at which Mr. H. preached. After the service we were introduced to several gentlemen of the civil service, who gave us some advice about our journey, and expressed much sympathy for us and interest in our mission.

As we walked back to the mission house, we remarked the havoc made on the premises by the mutineers. The chapel was built so solidly that it could not easily be destroyed, but by dint of great labor some of the pillars had been dislodged. Mr. Munnis's former house had been burned, at least the roof had, but the defaced and blackened walls were still standing.

When we arrived at the mission house, which was formerly occupied by Mr. and Mrs. Owen, we went to look at a great heap of broken furniture, demolished ware, etc., in fact the debris of Mr. Owen's once comfortable home. It was a gloomy sight; here a valuable book, now blackened and torn, there fragments of china and glass, and even part of the key-board of Mrs. Owen's piano, came to view.

Monday morning Mr. Munnis drove us down to the starting point of the cars, for as yet there was no station-house, but through a mistake we arrived just in time to see the train move off, so slowly, however, that if we had chosen we could have got on board without our baggage, which of course we did not choose to do. So we returned to the mission house, and improved the day in learning something of missionary work, and in listening to an account of the mutiny at that place. One incident occasioned us some amusement.

An engine stood alone on the railway, and the sepoys wishing to demolish it as something essentially feringhee in its character, yet being a little afraid of it as well, gathered some bricks and clubs, and commenced pelting the luckless engine with right good will. But conceive their alarm when it fairly began to move! They ran away, shouting, "Wuh Shaitan hai," (it is Satan.)

The engine, which only moved from the impetus their assault gave it, remained stationary thereafter, but they dared not touch it, and it was found uninjured when the English troops arrived.

Tuesday morning we were in time for the train, and did as we had been told, that is, took possession of some seats, saying "nothing to nobody."

Do you ask why we did not buy tickets like honest people? For this reason: the conductor had no right to sell us tickets, as none but people in government employ are allowed to go up the country further than Benares at present. The conductor, however, seemed to understand that we were to be smuggled up the country, and did not question us.

We found our horse and garee ready for us at Cangor. The coachwan (as the natives have corrupted it) went up with us on the train, so having placed our baggage aboard, we were soon rattling again over the Grand Trunk Road.

This was our first experience of a horse dak, and we did not find it particularly pleasant.

The horses were exceedingly fractious, and no wonder, for they were jaded and bruised in a manner painful to behold. Upon first starting out they would balk and kick, back and rear, in the most frantic manner. The coachman and groom would first coax the animal, saying, "O, my brother, my brother, go forward;" but when moral suasion failed, (as it always did, I am sorry to say,) they would drag the wheels on to the horse's heels, then apply the whip with loud cries, until the poor creature, maddened with pain, would leap forward and run the whole stage, a distance of six miles. Then the same programme would be gone through with by the next horse.

We reached Cawnpore at two o'clock Wednesday morning, and told the coachman to take us to a hotel. We had eaten nothing but dry biscuits and sandwiches since Tuesday morning, and began very strongly to desire that delightful beverage "that cheers, but not inebriates." We were taken to a hotel kept by a native, and a bearer, with a most repulsive face, brought lights and showed us a room. The khansamah was called, and we ordered tea and toast. Meanwhile we relieved ourselves of the dust somewhat, and walked about. At four o'clock we again set forth.

I shall never forget the long, dreadful day that followed. The heat was intense. The roads were dusty, and crowded with bullock-carts piled up with cotton, military stores, etc., and pedestrians and every variety of native vehicle.

Occasionally, too, we met parties of rough-looking natives armed with tulwars, that is, native swords, and old muskets. Whenever we saw them coming we drew the garee doors closely together, and kept perfectly quiet.

Near evening we came to Mynpoorie, where we stopped and procured some refreshments, although it was a most dangerous locality; but we felt as if we should perish without. Again on and on through the long weary night. We expected to reach Agra early in the morning, but it seemed as if the horses had combined to prevent our doing so. The whole programme of kicking, plunging, etc., with variations, was gone through with by each horse in succession.

About mid-day, however, we approached the long, wretched bridge of boats which spans the Jumna. Mr. Butler was to meet us in Agra, and had directed us to a palace called the Taj Mahal, and its dazzling dome and minarets soon blessed our vision. There we found not only our superintendent, but Mr. and Mrs. Pierce also.

Some well-furnished rooms in a building to the right of the Taj, called the Juwab, had been kindly vacated for us by the Rev. Mr. Evans and lady, who had meanwhile gone to stay with some friends in the fort. They left their servants and a nice dinner cooking for us. How we ate, rested, and refreshed ourselves generally I leave to your imagination. But I cannot forbear an attempt to describe that surpassingly lovely spot to you.

On the bank of the Jumna, just outside the city, and about a mile east from the fort, stands the "Taj Mahal," or crown palace, built by Shah Jahan, a celebrated Mogul king, who flourished about two centuries ago, for his beautiful queen Mumtaz Mahal, that is, the chosen of the palace. She was first buried in it, and afterward the king by her side. The building stands on an elevated platform, paved with marble laid in forms and smoothly joined. It is surrounded by a handsome balustrade, and there are two large marble basins for fountains; but they were not playing when we were there. There is a dome of purest white marble rising from the center of the palace, beneath which is the principal room containing the tombs. The floor of this room is of white marble, as are also the walls and the tombs; but all, except the floor, is closely inlaid with precious stones in vines and flowers. I counted in one small flower on one of the tombs twenty-seven differently colored stones.

You cannot imagine the singular beauty and brilliancy of this room. Words seem poor and tame when I attempt to describe it. At the entrance there is an arch, over and around which is also the inlaid work in precious stones. Besides every imaginable device and flower, it is stated that the whole of the Koran is thus inlaid upon those walls.

There are minarets at the outer angles of the walls, and many other ornaments that I need not describe. The dome, the room beneath it, and the entrance are the main objects of interest.

In the evening after our arrival Messrs. Scott and Williams, of the American Presbyterian Mission, came over from the fort, where the European residents still remain. They suggested that we all should go into the central room of the Taj and have an illumination, so we went over and ranged ourselves around the room. There are niches in the walls, in which were placed some wax candles. These were lighted simultaneously by native attendants, and the answering blaze of light from the walls and tombs was magnificent.

After we had admired the effect sufficiently we gathered around the tombs of the Mogul king and queen and sang the doxology. What would they not have done in the days of their power to one who dared to praise "Father, Son, and Holy Ghost" in their august presence?

To the left of the Taj stands a beautiful mosque, built of the red sandstone which is so much used in Agra. The building we occupied was built on the right of the Taj merely to preserve the symmetry of the whole, hence its name—the Juwab, or *answer*. The grounds are laid out with great care and skill, and present a great variety of trees, shrubs, and flowers.

Friday we all went over to the fort and examined the small space which the European residents of Agra fled to, and in which they remained during the fearfully hot and rainy seasons of 1857. It seems marvelous that no pestilence broke out among them. There was great suffering indeed, but it was in consequence of the lack of those conveniences and comforts which in this climate are necessities to Europeans.

There are some beautiful structures within the fort: the palace of Shah Jahan, his hall of audience, the Motee Musjid, or pearl mosque, and others. I was not able to visit these buildings, but the rest of our party did so, and returned in raptures.

Agra was formerly a large city. The old walls still remain, and extend along the Jumna about four miles in length, with a breadth of about three miles; but not even half of this space is occupied at present.

Toward evening our garees came to the gateway, and we again delivered ourselves over to the tender mercies of the coachwan and the redoubtable horseflesh of the Northwest Dak Company. We went forth without fear of Sepoys, however, for we had flanked the enemy, and emerged into comparative safety. The horses, too, seemed to feel better disposed toward us, and we went on without hinderance.

At early dawn we were roused from our slumbers by a confused mingling of shoutings, groanings of camels, neighing of horses, etc. One of our number seized his pistol before opening the door of his carriage, thinking it possible that the Sepoys had found us after all. He opened the door carefully, holding the revolver in advance, and confronted a twenty-four pounder drawn by a couple of huge elephants.

We soon discovered the cause of so much tumult. We were in the midst of General Penny's division, marching in to assist in the reoccupation of Rohilcund. We certainly wished him success, and that right speedily. After a fatiguing and monotonous day's journey we reached Mr. Butler's temporary residence in Meerut about eight o'clock P. M.

We are to remain here two or three weeks until the direct road through Rohilcund to Nynee Tal shall be open, and I seize this, the first leisure I have had since we left Benares, to write to the dear ones at home, who are, I know, anxiously waiting to hear of our welfare.

LETTER VI.

Departure from Meerut — Saharunpore — Deyrah Doon — Rajpore — Himalayas — Hill Vehicle — Hill Journey — April Fools — Acquisitions — Snowy Range — Rope Bridge — Teeree — Visit at the Rajah's Court — Scenery — Arrived at Nynee Tal.

NYNEE TAL, *May* 12, 1858.

MY DEAR MOTHER,—We concluded not to wait for the direct road to Nynee Tal to be opened, but determined instead to take a circuitous route by way of Saharunpore, Deyrah Doon, and Mussoorie, thence over the Sub-Himalayas, sixteen days' journey to Nynee Tal.

We left Meerut on the evening of the twenty-fourth of March. We journeyed by horse dak to Mozuffernugger, where we found a "kutchah" road, and were consequently obliged to travel in doolies the remainder of our journey to Deyrah Doon. A dooly is a substitute for a palkee. It is a frame covered with cloth instead of wood, which renders it much lighter than a palkee.

Our dust-covered doolies stopped at the premises of the American Presbyterian Missionaries in Saharunpore about mid-day of the twenty-fifth. We received a hearty welcome from

Rev. Dr. Campbell, a veteran missionary, and Mr. and Mrs. Calderwood. The latter have been in the country only about three years. Dr. Campbell's wife and children are on a visit to America.

We left Saharunpore at sunset, traveled all night, and at dawn crossed the Sewalik range of hills by a narrow, rocky defile, and emerged upon a level plateau called the Doon, or valley, a thousand feet higher than Saharunpore.

As the sun rose the high towering Himalayas were disclosed to our view, rising abruptly far up into the sky. They were truly magnificent, and there was something peculiarly pleasing in the contrast between their fresh green appearance and the dusty, parched plain.

We arrived at Deyrah Doon about mid-day, and found comfortable rooms ready for us at Mr. Williams's hotel. Mrs. Pierce and her babe (which was quite ill at Meerut) were both suffering from the fatigue of the journey, and Mr. H. and myself were both so ill that we were obliged to call a physician. It was therefore thought best to remain a few days and recruit our failing strength.

Those of our party who were able to go out attended service at the house of the American Presbyterian Missionaries on the Sabbath. The next day Mr. and Mrs. Woodside of that mission called and invited us to spend the day with them. As we were all improved in health we accepted the invitation, and spent a delightful day at the Mission-house. They have a fine site, and a commodious double house, occupied by two families—Mr. and Mrs. Woodside, and Mr. and Mrs. Herron.

Tuesday we drove up to Rajpore, a distance of six miles. It is merely a cluster of buildings quite at the foot of the mountains, the property of Mr. Haseltine. He was formerly a sergeant in the English army, and was in the expedition to Burmah at the time of the imprisonment of Judson and others, and saw those missionaries and the heroic Mrs. Judson after their release. His hotel is much frequented by people on their way to the hills, as just above it on the mountain slopes are the Sanitaria, Landour, and Mussoorie.

We had a busy time at Rajpore engaging hill men and hill vehicles to transport us to Nynee Tal. The former are shorter and hardier in their appearance than the people of the plains; the latter, called jhaumpauns, are very comfortable, and admirably adapted to hill traveling. A jhaumpaun is a chair with cane seat and back, and a platform with a railing round it for the feet. On either side are long poles fastened on with iron hooks. Straps of strong leather connect these poles near their ends, and in the middle of these straps a strong piece of wood, flat and about two feet in length, is securely fastened. Two men in front and two behind the chair stand either side of the cross pieces of leather, and each places one end of the flat stick on his shoulder. Their hands are left free to hold on to the poles, and thus they carry the vehicle. Four men more are always required on a long journey, in order to relieve the others. There is a top with curtains over the chair.

There were some dandas along, too, for some of the women servants. A danda is composed of a piece of strong cloth about two yards in length, fastened at either end to a strong pole. The cloth is gathered into a small compass and bound with leather, and fastened with rings of iron at either end of the pole. In the center of one side of the cloth another piece is sewed on endwise. On the opposite end of this piece is a strap, which also is fastened to either end of the pole. The person sits in the main piece of cloth, the smaller piece forming a place for the feet, and the straps being then buckled tightly, brings the cloth up as a covering to the feet and limbs. The pole comes front to the chest, and there are strong iron hooks in it, to which one may cling when the path is more perpendicular than pleasant. There is another broad strap which supports the back. It has a swinging motion, not very pleasant at first, but to which one soon becomes accustomed. It is safer than a jhaumpaun, and is carried by two men, with two for relief.

We were quite a cavalcade when we left Rajpore the last day of March. First went fifty or sixty men with baggage, that is, tents, cooking utensils, boxes of provisions, etc. Next the three "sahibs" on hill ponies, then the three jhaumpauns containing the "mem sahibs," and lastly the ayahs, or native woman servants.

Joel, our native preacher, was with us. He had a marvelous escape in the mutiny. He and his wife fled from Bareilly to Lucknow, and finding the mutiny had spread there also, they made their way as best they could to Allahabad. They were stopped several times and questioned. Joel was asked, "Are you a Mussulman or a Hindoo? You do not look like either." He invariably answered, "I am neither a Hindoo nor Mussulman, I am a Christian." Strange to say, they were not molested, but arrived safely in Allahabad and gained the fort.

Joel left his family in Allahabad and joined us in Meerut. He is a noble man, tall, and of pleasing person and manners. He is a good representative of Hindoostanee Christians. May there soon be many like him!

I have not mentioned the acquisitions we made at Deyrah-Doon. We found a native Christian woman there in distress. She was a faithful ayah or nurse in a gentleman's family, but her husband was intemperate and had in a fit of intoxication beaten her, and consequently had been forbidden the premises. The mistress of the poor woman allowed her to leave, that she might go with her husband, who will, we hope, "turn over a new leaf" in our mission. Samuel and Bella had been baptized by a missionary of the English Church, but it is doubtful if they understand much of Christianity. We hope they may be led to understand, and be made partakers of its spirit.

Imagine us winding up the narrow mountain paths, with the steep hill on one side, and the dark ravine on the other. The scenery was grand, magnificent, the grandeur and magnificence of nature lifting the thoughts of the Christian beholder directly up to the great Creator. Man had no part in piling those lofty summits and clothing them with beauty; it was the work of God!

We passed through the single street or bazar of Landour about mid-day, and admired the pleasant houses situated on the adjacent slopes. We had left the place well in our rear, when our coolies halted and requested us to have our tents pitched in a fine situation which they pointed out. True, it was not yet night, but they had not purchased sufficient flour, etc., to meet their wants until they could be able to procure more.

Their story, however, was not credited, and they were bade to go on. Our tents were pitched at last in a most exposed situation on the brow of a mountain. In the night the winds blew terrifically, and threatened to carry off our tents; but by dint of great care they were kept in their places.

April 1st dawned cold and rainy, and we arose to find ourselves as precious a set of April fools as need be. Not a coolie could be found! all had gone quietly back to Landour to purchase their provisions, and we could do nothing but await their return with what patience we might. It was a dismal day, followed by a most wretched night. The next morning the coolies were in readiness to attend us, and when reprimanded for leaving the day previous only laughed, and said, "You could not expect us to carry you and your goods if we had nothing to eat." Ah! I can never forget the discomforts of that terrible journey. We became accustomed to the rugged heights and deep valleys; to climbing the one and being suspended over the other; to cold chilling winds on the one, and steamy, stifling heat in the other. We became familiar with early breakfasts, cold luncheon at mid-day, and dinner at nine o'clock P. M.

Now that I have given you a passing glimpse of the shady side of our journey, I must try and show you the sunny side as well. We certainly had some magnificent views, and none were more so than those of the snowy ranges of the Himalayas.

The average elevation of the Himalayas is from eighteen to twenty thousand feet above the sea level. The limit of perpetual snow on the southern slopes is from fifteen to eighteen thousand feet. Some of the highest peaks are from twenty-five to twenty-eight thousand feet above the level of the sea. The white glistening glaciers seemed to lose themselves in the heavens, and could at times be distinguished from the clouds only by their superior brilliancy. Sometimes the clouds concealed them wholly from our view, then, parting suddenly, disclosed an apparent city of glittering pinnacles and towers of dazzling whiteness. I was often reminded of Revelation xxi, 10: "And he carried me away in the spirit to a great and high mountain, and showed me that great city, the holy Jerusalem, descending out of heaven from God."

The first Sabbath was a welcome day, and we all improved it by resting. Toward evening we met in the largest tent and held a class and prayer meeting.

The succeeding week we entered the little native kingdom of Teeree, and crossed the stream, that flowed through a deep gorge near the capital, on a rope bridge. We found some

European gentlemen measuring the distance across the stream, and making plans for a suspension bridge, so we presumed the ropes had not been very recently renewed.

We went over on this wise. A man went ahead to open the bridge, which had railings of woven ropes, floor ditto, interlaced with sticks. One at a time we were carried over in a danda, the bridge closing behind us. When in the center, the swaying motion was extremely unpleasant; but the hill men did not seem to mind it at all. They almost ran back each time with the empty danda, but they were very careful with us.

Having safely crossed, we turned from the road to the left, and passing through the little village, pitched our tents on the bank of the river, which at that point forms a bow. Close by our tents stood a large hollow tree. Fifteen men could stand in the cavity at once. Our servants used it for a storeroom for our boxes of provisions, kettles, etc. Soon after our arrival there came a deputation from the Rajah of Teeree to present a nuzzer, (gift,) according to eastern custom. It consisted of a large number of rupees, some sugar, rice, and a large goat. We only retained the goat, which was at once slain, and distributed among our servants. We touched the money and the other articles with the tips of our fingers, to signify that we accepted the courtesy of the rajah, and they were taken back. Joel was of course our interpreter and master of ceremonies upon this occasion. Afterward the gentlemen and Joel went up to a little round open pavilion on the brow of a hill near us, and paid their respects to the rajah. There was considerable attempt at display on his part, in a ludicrously impoverished and barbaric style. Little bells were rung, speeches were made, questions asked and answered, and profound salams made upon parting.

We went on our way next morning and met new objects of interest as we proceeded. The mountain slopes were more generally cultivated than at first, and were occasionally dotted with small villages. The houses were built of stone, roofed with saplings, over which thin flat stones were put on in layers, the edges overlapping like shingles.

Men, women, and children often ran out to look at us. Their clothing looked warm, but was very dirty, and their tangled and matted hair hung loosely about their necks. I noticed, however, that their features were very good, and their forms strong and well developed.

The chrysanthemum and cactus that we cherish so carefully in America grow wild on these hills, and in great profusion. The cactus grows to a mammoth size, forming awkward-looking shrubs and trees.

But the rhododendron bears the palm among the trees of the mountains. It is large, and rather ungraceful in shape, with its trunk and branches generally covered with silvery moss. The foliage is of a rich dark green, and very luxuriant. The rhododendrons were now in blossom, and the flowers were splendid. They are more like the peony than any other flower I can think of.

We expected to be obliged to cross the Ganges at Seereenugger on another rope bridge, but found to our great delight that an iron suspension bridge had just been completed there. As we passed over the beautiful structure we called Teeree to mind, and felt most sensibly our indebtedness to civilization.

Another Sabbath of quiet rest and worship, another week of toilsome journeyings. We often found the road quite swept away by the rains of the preceding year, since which the usual repairs had not been made, and we were several times obliged to leave the main road and go by the "pug dundees," or by-paths.

Saturday evening came, and we were still some distance from Nynee Tal. The darkness increased, and the men who carried the jhaumpauns were in great trepidation lest by some misstep they should precipitate the mem sahibs into the yawning depths. I leave you to imagine the frame of mind enjoyed by the mem sahibs themselves. The gentlemen, foot-sore and weary, clambered along on the edge of the road and steadied the jhaumpauns. The ponies had long since given out, and were either left behind or were scarcely able to drag themselves along. The darkness increased, and the coolies attempted to improvise torches, but did not succeed.

Finally, after several "hair-breadth escapes," we gained the top of the mountain, and looked over into a valley that just then seemed to us the most desirable spot on earth. From various points lights were gleaming in the windows of white cottages, now dusky in the overshadowing forests, and far down below we could discern the still waters of Nynee Tal.

We were met by Mr. Parsons, a member of our mission, whom we had not previously seen. He came to us from a mission of the Church of England in this country. We remained at his house that night. Mr. Pierce and family went home with Mr. Butler, whose two little boys had been left in the hills when they went down to Meerut, so that they had a home in readiness to receive them.

The next day was the first Sabbath which we spent within the limits of our mission field, and as we looked back and reviewed the anxieties, troubles, and dangers of the previous six months, our hearts were filled with gratitude to Him who had delivered us out of them all.

In the evening we attended an English service in Mr. Butler's parlor. The room was filled mostly with ladies. There were only two or three gentlemen present, besides those of our own party, as the officers who took refuge here last year have rejoined the army. Mr. Butler had rented houses for us, and we immediately addressed ourselves to the task of setting them in order. They were furnished, and the floors were covered with the thin cotton carpeting manufactured in the North-west.

We found it a difficult task to procure suitable servants, and teach them to perform their duties, for there are no trained servants here, as in Calcutta. We are obliged to keep four men as jhaumpanees, that is, men to carry me in the jhaumpaun, or danda, as I cannot walk very far up hill, and we cannot go out to walk without having a hill to climb. They also fetch our wood and water, and grass for the pony.

I will not attempt to tell you anything more of Nynee Tal at present, except to say that it is a delightful little eyrie-like place, but will wait till I shall have seen more of it.

Rohilcund has been retaken, the principal

cities occupied by English troops, and the postal and transportation arrangements re-organized.

We heard yesterday that our boxes have all safely arrived at Kaleedoongee, at the foot of the hills, so we shall soon have a busy time in unpacking.

Mission Premises at Nynee Tal.

LETTER VII.

Nynee Tal — Nynee Davee — Mount Chenar — Daily Routine — Girls' School — Boys' School — Mrs. Parsons — Blunders — Orphan Boys.

NYNEE TAL, *June* 15, 1858.

MY DEAR MOTHER,—Nynee Tal is a little undulated valley completely encircled by mountains, itself six thousand five hundred feet above the level of the sea. The mountains around it rise two thousand feet higher. The little lake which gives the place its name occupies the lower part of the valley, and is only three fourths of a mile in length, and scarcely half a mile in width. The higher part of the valley is occupied by the native bazar, beyond which it extends but a short distance, and ends in a low hill, on the top of which stands "St. John's in the wilderness," the picturesque English church.

There is just room sufficient for a road eight or ten feet wide around the lake, part of which was made by excavating the hill-slopes.

All around on the mountain sides are tasteful white cottages, built of wood and stone, and much more resembling our dwellings at home than the houses on the plains.

At the head of the lake, embowered in large willows, stands a tiny Hindoo temple, dedicated to the worship of a goddess whom they call Nynee Davee. She is represented as the wife of Sheev, or Mahesh the destroyer, the third person in the Hindoo triad. Nynee simply means little. She, or rather it, is a little inferior figure, about ten inches in height, clothed with a woman's dress, the figure and dress both being carved out of stone. We went to see it one day. A well-to-do-looking priest met us at the doors of the temple, and when we asked permission to see the idol replied in the affirmative with profound salams. I could not forbear saying to him, "Will you please ask the idol to come to the door?"

The Brahmin only laughed; but upon my repeating the question he said, "She cannot walk to the door."

"Not walk to the door!" I repeated. "Can she walk at all?"

"No, mem sahib," said he with a conscious leer.

"She is not a very powerful being I should think," said I, "and I think it is great nonsense to worship any being who is weaker than we are."

He only laughed as before, and we went in and saw the idol in its place of honor. Worship had just concluded, I suppose, as the little figure had a yellow skirt tied on over its stone dress, and its head was wet, as if water had just been poured over it. There were some remains of rice and flowers lying in front of her, probably part of the morning offerings.

To the right of the temple the road leads through the bazar, and on past several cottages till it terminates by the church. There are smooth, hard roads winding about the beautiful mountains quite to their tops, and the loveliness that meets the eye at every point cannot be adequately described.

The dells are rich in many varieties of fern and moss, interspersed with wild flowers, and the slopes are covered with trees—firs, oaks, maples, rhododendrons, and many others. Black and orange raspberries grow in some localities in profusion.

Till the last of June the climate of the hills is delightful. We improved it this season in taking long walks and rides every morning, gaining in health and vigor daily in the clear, bracing atmosphere.

Occasionally we all met at some appointed place and breakfasted together in the open air. We breakfasted one morning on the top of Chenar, the highest point near Nynee Tal. It is eight thousand seven hundred and fifty feet above the sea level. From the top we could look down on the far-reaching plains on the one hand, and up to the towering snow-mountains on the other. The first glaciers are about one hundred miles distant from Nynee Tal by the mountain road, but much nearer in a straight line.

As they are from fifteen to twenty thousand feet higher than Chenar, they seemed that morning to be within a day's journey. We remained wrapt in admiration, gazing upon the glittering domes and spires of an apparent city of light up there in the clouds, until the morning sun vailed its supernatural loveliness with a curtain of amber haze. Just then, too, our khansamah announced the fact that breakfast was ready, and although it seemed too magnificent a spot to desecrate by the commonplace act of eating, yet as our appetites were keen after our long ride in the bracing morning air, when we found an inviting repast spread on a snowy cloth over the grassy table, we did not hesitate to do it full justice.

On our way down we saw a few large baboons sitting on the lower branches of some trees, and gravely regarding us. Whether they were considering how long it would be in the ordinary course of transmigration before they could dwell in similar forms to ours, or wondering at our intrusion, I really cannot say.

Another favorite place of resort is called the

landslide. Part of a mountain seems to have slidden down through a deep chasm. On the bank overlooking this chasm the view is sublime; but we can only spend a little time in explorations, merely enough to insure ourselves needful recreation.

The language still looms up before us as a great mountain that we have just begun to climb.

We have not had an efficient moonshee since we came to Nynee Tal. Joel assists us all he can; but as he and Mr. Parsons are the only ones to carry on the boys' school, which was opened in May, and to preach to the natives, we do not like to call on him very much. This has been a great drawback to our progress, since, study as we may, we cannot be sure that we are always pronouncing the words of our lesson right.

Now shall I give you an account of our daily routine? We rise at half past five, and as soon as we are dressed have our chotahaziree, or little breakfast, which is composed of tea and toast. We then walk down to the foot of the lake, probably a mile from our door; then Mr. H. on his hill pony, and I in my danda, climb some one of the hill paths, and make our way home about seven o'clock. We then have prayers, after which we study our Hindoostanee lessons until nine o'clock, when the cook comes to the study door and says, "Haziree taiyar hai;" that is, Breakfast is ready.

One table is supplied with good beef, mutton, fowls, vegetables, bread, milk, and butter. This last is peculiar to the hills. We can also generally procure fruit.

After breakfast I give out material for dinner from the storeroom, and directions how to have it prepared. This course is usually practiced here to prevent the cooks from using more than is needful; but they frequently take revenge by tolling what is given them quite heavily, and sometimes they make a great mistake, and cook the toll for our dinner, while they keep the principal themselves.

I always remonstrate when such a mistake is made, and the worthy Mohammedan says in reply, as he piously folds his hands, "Mem sahib, I am astonished you should think me capable of such baseness! I, who eat your honor's salt!" that is, who get my food by your honor's service. I then admonish him that if he does not keep to his salt and let superfluities alone I shall surely subtract the price of whatever is taken from his wages. After such a scene he generally walks warily for about ten days.

After the giving out of dinner is completed I join Mr. H. in the study, and we read our lessons and translate them till twelve, when I usually go to the girls' school, which is held in a room of Mr. Pierce's house. I suppose you may think we cannot teach native children much about their own language yet, but you are mistaken; they often speak their own language very incorrectly, and scarcely ever know a single letter.

There are fifteen girls in the school, the children of our own servants and those of European residents. Besides these there are several women, servants and wives of servants, who are learning to read. We teach them the Ten Commandments, the Lord's Prayer, and various hymns, by rote; also explain to them portions of Scripture daily. Some of them learn to read Hindoostanee, others Roman-Urdu, or Hindoostanee in the Roman character, and others Hindee. The last hour of school is devoted to sewing, knitting, crocheting, etc.

We use the hymn book of the American Presbyterian Mission, which is in the Roman-Urdu, as are also the few copies of the New Testament which we have been able to procure. Of course there was wholesale destruction of Christian books during the mutiny, and now but few copies can be obtained, but there will soon be plenty of them again.

I am obliged to give the children many wholesome admonitions to keep quiet and look on their books. A class sits around me in a half circle, and the little curious black eyes are continually glancing at my feet, dress, hair, and eyes, anywhere in fact but on the book which I hold in my hand. I sometimes say to them, "Here in this book are the letters, not on my head, nor dress; now observe this letter closely and see how it looks, what is it?" Their attention is thus gained for a few moments. I return home in time to dress for dinner, (a proceeding doubly necessary after contact with the children,) which is served at three o'clock.

After dinner we write letters, and study Forbes's grammar until near evening, when we again sally forth to "eat the air," as the Hindoostanee phrase is. In the evening we frequently have religious services, either in Hindoostanee or English, and sometimes meet for a social visit. Every Monday morning we meet and breakfast together, the missionaries first discussing matters supposed to be too deep for us; but usually they bring up again at the breakfast table the questions they have discussed and settled.

On the Sabbath we have Hindoostanee services in the morning, and an English sermon at five o'clock P. M. At the former Mr. Parsons and Joel alternate, and the other missionaries at the latter. The Hindoostanee services are held in a room which we have fitted up for that purpose, but which was formerly a sheep-house. Two services during the week are held at the barracks for the benefit of the invalid soldiers. Several among them are Christians, and others are seeking the Saviour. We have very interesting meetings with them.

There are about twenty boys in attendance at the bazar school. There were many objections made by the boys' parents to prayers being held in the school. One man, more alarmed than the others, came to Mr. Parsons and said he should take his boy out if the Bible were read and prayer offered in the school any more. "Do you suppose," asked Mr. Parsons, "that we are such ungrateful people that we will commence our daily labor without thanking God for taking care of us, and asking his blessing upon our work. You Hindoos are very scrupulous about your daily worship, and do you think Christians should be less so?" No, the man thought not, but the teachers might have their worship at home before coming to school. Mr. Parsons told him they did have family worship, but they considered it also their duty to have prayers in the school. The man went away dissatisfied, but did not withdraw his son.

Mr. Parsons terrified a rather unruly boy one day by telling him that if he behaved so badly again he should "kill him outright." He meant to say he should *beat* him.

We all make ludicrous mistakes at times. One told a bearer to fetch a "little girl," and put her on the fire! The servant stared in amazement, and the gentleman perceiving his error, called for a little "lukree," wood, instead of "lurkee," a girl. A lady told her servant to give her little daughter a small "basket" of chicken for dinner! instead of a small "piece." She used the word tokra instead of tukra.

Another told her cook to boil some goorgas (a class of warlike people) for dinner, meaning gajars, that is, carrots. So we must go on, blundering and rectifying blunders, until the thick darkness that envelops the language shall wear away. We begin already to see through the intricacies which have perplexed us so much, and with "sabar karo" (literally, make patience) for our motto, we hope to emerge into the light by and by.

Mr. Parsons and Joel preach in the main street of Nynee Yal and at the foot of the lake every week. They have many hearers, who listen with apparent eagerness and delight to the message of salvation; but at this date only one has decided to break the chains of heathenism and become a disciple of the Lord Jesus Christ.

Meanwhile we hope the work of grace is going on in the hearts of the few native Christians with us. Joel declares that he has recently experienced such a change in his heart, and obtained such light and joy in the Lord, as he never had before. Samuel and Bella are improving also, and seem to apprehend more fully the power of the Christian religion to purify the heart and life.

We have three orphan boys in charge. The oldest, who is about twelve years of age, is from the plains. He is the son of a Sepoy who was slain in the mutiny. He was found wandering about a village by Captain Gowan, who took him in charge and made him over to Mr. Butler while he was in Meerut. Captain Gowan is to support the boy so long as it shall be necessary. He is called James Gowan, after his benefactor. Such "loot," that is, plunder, is surely far preferable to the diamonds and cashmere shawls taken in Delhi.

The other two boys are paharees, bright and keen as their own mountain air. They were original specimens of humanity when they were first brought to our mission by a poor leper woman. Their clothing consisted of a tattered black woolen blanket each, their long hair was thickly tangled, and they were, of course, covered with vermin. They are considerably more civilized in appearance now. Their heads have been shaved, and comfortable though coarse garments provided for them.

The elder boy is supported also by Captain G., and is named Thomas Gowan. The other is called William Wheeler. He is a remarkably bright-looking and sweet-voiced lad, and bids fair to be a great favorite. Bella has them all in charge, and assists them to cook their simple meals.

It is full time for the rains to begin falling. Ominous lowering clouds hover about the mountain tops, in apparent readiness to dispense their favors, and we must soon exchange this bright sunshine and balmy air for fogs and showers. Ah! well,

> "Into each life some rain must fall,
> Some days must be dark and dreary."

LETTER VIII.

Rainy Season — Laying Corner-stone of First Mission Chapel — Removal of two Families to Lucknow — Eurasian Moonshee and wife — Mr. H. begins to preach in Hindoostanee — A Laughable Mistake.

NYNEE TAL, Jan. 20, 1859.

MY DEAR MOTHER,—The rain commenced falling the last week in June, and spoiled our delightful home-like summer weather. It continued for nearly three months with but little intermission, and we were in consequence obliged to stay within doors most of the time. Of course our health was affected by such close confinement. All of us, indeed, suffered more or less in the course of the season, and two or three of our number were quite seriously ill.

We have, however, made considerable advancement in our studies. We can read quite readily now in the Persi-Arabic character. There are thirty-five characters in all. Twenty-four of these have three forms—the initial, medial, and final. Three have but two forms, and eight do not change at all.

We have also learned the Hindee alphabet, and commenced reading short stories in that language. As the verbs are like the Hindoostanee, of which it is the basis, I think we can learn it quite readily. The Urdu, or Hindoostanee, is made up from the Hindee, Arabic, and Persian languages, and makes, as was its design, a sort of universal language throughout a large part of India.

During the season a subscription paper was circulated among the European residents of Nynee Tal, in order to procure means to build a chapel and school-house on a lot which had been secured for mission premises, and a sufficient sum having been realized to warrant us in commencing work, we all met one morning in the first week of October to lay the corner-stone of our first mission chapel.

Major Ramsay, commissioner of this district, who takes a deep interest in our work and has subscribed liberally for it, laid the corner-stone, after which the masons prepared several stones, and each member of the mission laid one in the foundation. We then sang a hymn, prayer was offered, and we went away. The natives looked wonderingly on, and must have thought an unusual building was to be erected. We hope it may be a place to which many of them shall love to resort.

Immediately after this incident Mr. Butler and Mr. Pierce, with their families, and Joel, removed to Lucknow, in the province of Oude, to commence a mission in that city. It was a long and trying journey for them all, but particularly so for Mrs. Pierce, who had but just recovered from a severe illness. They arrived safely at Lucknow, and are now occupying a large building which was formerly the residence of a begum or native princess. It is called Asfee Kotee, and although built in native style, is quite comfortable. In November the house on our recently purchased mission premises in Nynee Tal was vacated, and we moved into it. It is a long low building, evidently intended for two families. In the center are two parlors exactly alike. The front of each room is covered with glass put in sashes quite down to the floor. Either side of the parlors are two large and two small rooms.

The house is very comfortable this winter, but I fear it will not be waterproof in the rainy season. It is known as "The Ruin." We are told that it was built by contract, and when finished was condemned. It certainly has not grown more substantial since. We occupy half the house, and the other part is occupied by Mr. Knowles and family, who have recently come up from Meerut and joined our mission. Mr. Knowles was in the English army, but has been led to devote his life to the missionary work.

Our girls' school was given up in October, as most of the children left with their parents either for the plains or the teräee about that time. The teräee is a belt of jungle or wild land at the foot of the mountains.

Many of the paharees go down and cultivate fields in the teräee during the winter months, while their own mountain lands are covered with snow. On this account our boys' school is very small. Probably, when our mission here is firmly established, the school will be removed during the winter months to some point adjacent to the teräee.

December 1st we had a fine snow-storm, which seemed quite home-like of course. The snow has not wholly disappeared from the mountains since, but we have bright pleasant weather. We have fireplaces in our rooms, and as wood is abundant we keep very comfortable. My health is greatly improved since the close of the rainy season. I walk a mile and a half often, and feel nearly as strong as ever.

We have had an excellent moonshee for about two months, but he has just left us for government employ. He is a Eurasian, that is, of mixed descent. In 1857 he became a Mussulman to save his life. He went to a place called Casseepore, in an independent native state, and while there he became very intimately acquainted with a wealthy Mohammedan physician, who even admitted him to his house and allowed him to see his wife. She was his only wife, and remarkably intelligent and lovely.

After a while the physician suddenly died, and the wily Eurasian managed to appropriate both his widow and wealth. The latter, however, seems either to have been inconsiderable, or else has taken to itself wings and flown away, but the lady (for she is a lady) was here with her husband. She is a finished Urdu scholar, and a most efficient teacher. She has assisted me while here in the Hindoostanee, and in return I have taught her to read in Roman-Urdu. She wishes to become a Christian, and is a constant student of the Bible. I was deeply interested in her, and regretted that she was obliged to leave. She is altogether quite a different specimen of womanhood from those I have hitherto met in India. She is no darker complexioned than many American ladies, and has the beautiful almond-shaped eye and soft dark hair which belong to Oriental countries. She is of medium height and good proportions, and moves with a singularly graceful air. I suppose she is a type of those ladies who are so closely secluded from observation by the high walls which form so prominent a part of every Mohammedan gentleman's residence.

A few days after they left us we received a letter which explained the reason why he had felt so ill at ease in our mission. The letter was from one of the missionaries at Deyrah Doon, and informed us that Thomas Orr (for that was his name) had rather an aged wife in that place! He had left her wholly without means, judging rightly that the missionaries would not allow her to suffer; but since he was in our employ they desired a portion of his salary to be forwarded regularly for her support.

Mr. Humphrey has been preaching in Hindoostanee occasionally for some time; on a very small scale, he says, but still it is a beginning. I hope by spring, when we expect to open a mission in Bareilly, he will be able to preach without much embarrassment. Experienced missionaries tell us, however, that we cannot become proficient in the language in less than four years.

On the first week of January Mr. Parsons moved down to Moradabad, and as he could not obtain a house, is living in tents. We are to join him there soon, and remain until a house can be obtained in Bareilly.

Ladies are still prohibited residing in Rohilcund; but it is expected that the prohibition will soon be removed, as it is quite safe to live in any station in the province.

It is indeed wonderful with what rapidity the country becomes quiet. No sooner are English troops in possession of a city, and the rebel Sepoys dispersed or imprisoned, than law and order resume their wonted course throughout the entire district.

Native Christians of Nynee Tal.

There is some dismay on the part of our servants, as they do not like to go to the plains, they are so afraid of the heat, nor do they like to lose their situations.

Nundoo, a strict Hindoo, who came to us as jhaumpaunee, has risen to the post of house bearer, and as his wages are increased a little thereby he does not like to fall from the height to which he has attained. I had a vast deal of trouble in teaching him to dust furniture, trim the lamps, etc., for which he seems very grateful. He tells us often we are his ma-bap, that is, parents. Ma-bap is a title often bestowed by natives on Europeans who are kind to them or whom they wish to propitiate.

Nundo being wholly unaccustomed to European houses, sometimes makes egregious mistakes about the nature of things. He places the books back on the shelves, after dusting them, wrong side up with care; and after he has arranged the beds, the flowers on the counterpane all point gracefully toward the foot!

When we moved into this house he managed everything very well, but after some days I recollected that a china spittoon was missing. It had never been used, and as it generally stood on the window-sill in my dressing room, Nundoo supposed it to be a rare sort of vase, so he had placed it carefully in my bonnet-box, under my best bonnet! When I made inquiry, and he gravely disclosed its safe lodging place, he was greeted by a burst of laughter that greatly embarrassed him. He looked at us in surprise, which was not diminished when we informed him of the designed use of the article.

We have another orphan boy, whom we obtained in a singular manner. A gentleman was riding leisurely along by the lake one day, when he heard some unusual noises, as of crying or groaning. They seemed to proceed from under the road, so he called his sais, or groom, to see if there were a channel under the road, as there often is for the rills that run down the mountain sides to reach the lake without flooding the road. He found a channel, and in it a little boy bent almost double. He pulled him out and tried to ascertain who he was, and how he came there; but the child did not utter a word, and seemed paralyzed with fright. The gentleman brought him to us, and we handed him over to Bella's kind care. For two weeks he remained speechless, although he often seemed to wish to speak. Meanwhile we ascertained that he was an orphan, with no friend who cared to claim him, and that his name was Gulab Sing, a very common Hindoo name. He had been living with a married sister who treated him harshly, and it was through fear of her that he took refuge in the channel.

Soon as it became evident that he would remain with us, I made him some new clothes. Till then he had worn some old clothing of the other boys. When he first saw his new suit he spoke right out, "These are mine," and since that time he answers whenever spoken to, but rarely speaks of his own accord.

On Christmas day we thought we would like to attend the communion service at the English Church, but were refused permission to do so by Mr. Hinde, the present chaplain. Is it not astonishing that such bigotry still exists in the Christian Church?

Before this letter shall reach you we expect to be settled in Bareilly. You shall be duly informed of our progress in the work, and of all incidents of sufficient interest to write, if my health continues good.

LETTER IX.

Journey to Moradabad—Garden—Bazar Preaching—Call from the Sikhs—Visit at their Villages—Mission House pro tem.—Mr. H. goes to Bareilly—Removal there—Servants—Cashmere Kotee—Native Assistants—Hindoo Festivals.

BAREILLY, April 10, 1859.

MY DEAR MOTHER,—We left Nynee Tal January 25th, and reached Moradabad the next morning. We found the distance from Nynee Tal to Kaleedoongee, at the foot of the hills, to be fourteen miles of romantic mountain scenery.

We stopped at the little dak bungalow at Kaleedoongee for an hour or two, and then arranged our palkees for the night journey. Mine was a comfortable hired palkee, but Mr. Humphrey's arrangements in that line were rather unusual. He took a light bedstead, (our only one,) which was innocent of posts, merely having four feet and frame covered with wide cotton tape woven like basket work, placed it on the ground in an inverted position, bound four strips of wood to the four feet and fastened them together, forming a gable at each end. A strong pole was then fastened across to the top of each gable, and the ends left projecting like the handles of a palkee. Over this frame my album quilt was placed, and being duly sewed together at the ends, with the exception of a small opening for ingress and egress, formed a miniature movable tent. Altogether it looked so comical that we fairly astonished the misty jungles with our peals of laughter, and their leafy labyrinths rang again with the echoes.

We found our kahars all present at each station, and so went on right merrily. As night waned toward the small hours, my kahars ran so far ahead with me that my husband's crazy vehicle was wholly lost sight of. I knew nothing of it, however, until my palkee stopped suddenly, and I heard voices in altercation.

"We have a mem sahib inside," were the first words I distinguished.

"No you haven't," said several voices at once, "a mem sahib wouldn't be traveling alone nowadays."

"She is not," replied my men; "the sahib himself is only a little way behind."

"Well," said the others, "you can't go on until he comes."

My kahars were loth to wait, as they were anxious to arrive at the end of the stage, and have a good smoke together before the other's arrival, so they sent one of their number to confer with me. He came to the palkee door and said, "Mem sahib, will your honor please to look out and let the soldiers see that you are really an English mem sahib?"

I confess I was a little startled, for I could not hear the name "sepoy" without a shudder. I slid back the door, however, and inquired boldly of the kahars if the sahib were near. They answered, "Not far off."

Just then a band of armed native soldiers pressed up to my palkee, and looked sharply at me.

I said to them, "Why have you stopped my palkee?"

One of the soldiers, who seemed the leader, stepped forward and replied that they were soldiers of the Nawab of Rampore, and were watching for Nana Sahib, who was supposed to be about making an attempt to escape to the interior by way of the nawab's territories, on the borders of which we then were. I was quite reassured at this, and waited very patiently till Mr. H. came up, when we were allowed to go on.

By and by we came to a river, and were taken through it by the kahars lifting the palkees on their shoulders high and dry. I supposed our trials for the night were all over, and was composing myself to sleep when I heard again the low plash of water. The men seemed to go in deeper and deeper, so I sat up and opened the doors.

A scene of singular loveliness met my eyes. Water was all around, placid and quiet as an infant's sleep. Far in the dim distance I could discern the shadowy shore, and there in the midst of the waters was my insignificant palkee, myself and kahars being apparently the only living objects on the scene. All was lighted up by the peculiarly soft moonlight of the Orient. Soon the water was so deep that I could reach it from the palkee, and the kahars kept shouting to each other, "Be careful, my brother; step carefully," etc. Soon they raised the palkee to their shoulders, and at last upon their heads. I did not feel very comfortable to be out at sea in such a guise. I prefer a ship for water-traveling decidedly. In a little while the men landed me safely on the "other shore," and set me down on the sand.

I then saw that Mr. Humphrey's dooly had not left the shore, but was set down on the opposite bank while his men assisted mine in bringing me over. My kahars then returned with his, and brought him over in the same manner.

I could not help indulging in another hearty laugh at the little three-cornered dooly as it loomed up so fantastically through the moonlight, perched on the kahars' heads. As soon as Mr. H. was set down by me the kahars ran together to a spot near by and kindled a fire with some dry twigs which they must have smuggled over somehow, perhaps on the top of my palkee. As the flames rose they all thrust their legs (they were not troubled with trowsers) right into them several times, withdrawing them dexterously, so as to dry but not burn them. We then proceeded on our way without further interruption.

The morning sun was pouring down floods of light, dispelling the mist that settles over the plains at night during the cold season, as we entered Moradabad.

Our kahars took us across the fields direct to cantonments, thus avoiding the long bridge, the dusty, noisy city, and the increasing heat. We arrived at Mr. Parsons's tents about nine o'clock A. M., where we found breakfast in waiting. A new era dawned upon us then and there. Delicious sweet potatoes, cauliflowers, oranges, and lemons, all showed us that we were again in India. It is strange that twenty-four hours' traveling can ever make such a difference, but so it does sometimes. We left midwinter in the mountains and found golden autumn in the plains.

We noticed, too, such a change in the appearance of the people. In Nynee Tal the natives were gloomy and stupid. Wrapped in large black woolen blankets, they passed most of their time in the enjoyment of the inevitable hookah, and seemed almost to have forgotten that work is a necessity.

The plains' folk, on the contrary, were all about the streets, alert and brisk, and intent upon prosecuting their several crafts. Here a cloth merchant, with a white mark on his forehead, to show that he had performed his pooja (idol worship) that day, was striding proudly along, while several kahars were carrying his huge bundles of dry goods to supply the wants of the mem sahibs; there a Cashmere merchant, looking every inch a Mussulman, with a large bundle of embroidered shawls and cloaks; here a gardener, with a flat basket covered with vegetables, fruit, and nuts, hastening to present his offering at the feet of some potential sahib; there a box-walla, or yankee-notion peddler; while fowls in baskets, game in netted bags, curiosities in carved wood and ivory, all had representative venders in the streets.

The evening succeeding our arrival in Moradabad Mrs. Parsons and I walked in a beautiful, though neglected garden, which, previous to the mutiny, had been kept up by the government authorities. This was the first time I had seen oranges and lemons on the trees, and certainly the sight was most lovely.

There were long rows of orange trees, each loaded with delicious fruit, though no two trees seemed to bear precisely the same kind. We found one tree that bore a very peculiar orange, to which we voted the palm. It was rather long, with a thin, smooth rind, and a strip of brown mossy bark around its center.

There were both sweet and sour lemons in abundance, but no other fruit was then ripe, although the peach, pomegranate, pear, fig, guava, custard-apple, and mango trees gave promise of great variety in the hot season. There was also a long row of plantains, which are perhaps more properly plants than trees. The plantain grows to the height of twelve or fifteen feet. There are usually several stalks growing close to each other, on which are immense leaves, often three or four feet in length and one or two in width. The strong fibers that vein the leaf keep it from being blown to fragments by the wind. As it is, they are often slit up so as to resemble a huge green feather. The leaves as well as the stalks droop considerably, which gives the plantain a singular and peculiar tropical appearance. On each of the large stalks there is a fruit. A smaller stalk leaves the main one at about two thirds its height, and droops over toward the ground. It is leafless, but at the end is a large red bud. The clusters of plantains form around this stalk in several places, perhaps four or five. They are about four inches in length and two around, of a sweet, mealy substance. The smaller kind, called the banana by Europeans, and which is so plentiful in Bengal and Southern India, is much superior in taste.

The missionaries were busy for a few days in looking up a house, and at last succeeded in finding one that could be rented.

Mr. H. accompanied Mr. Parsons to the city for bazar preaching several times, and found he could express his thoughts in Hindoostanee even in the crowded, busy streets.

One day, to our great surprise, a deputation of men from some villages about twenty miles to the south of Moradabad visited us, and requested the missionaries to visit their people, and teach them the doctrines of the Christian faith. They were of a class of people called the Muzhubee Sikhs. They stated that there was a desire among their people to forsake the Hindoo religion wholly and worship the true God. We asked them how they knew anything about the true God. They answered that they had heard the Padre sahibs from the southern side of the Ganges preach the Gospel at the annual melas, or religious fairs, on the banks of that river; and that many of their learned men had received small books from them that told of a Saviour, one both divine and human, who had of his own free will made atonement for the sins of men in his own person by suffering and death; that he rose from the dead, and that all who believe in him shall be saved from their sins and inherit everlasting happiness. "We feel," said they, "that this is just what we want; this religion is exactly suited to our case."

Probably the missionaries referred to were those of Futteghur, who were slaughtered at Cawnpore. They have gone to join those who, like themselves, were slain "for the word of God, and the testimony which they held;" but their memory is precious, and the seed they sowed in tears is now springing up in beauty and promise.

Mr. Parsons and Mr. Humphrey went out to the villages on an appointed day. They arrived in the evening, and found about forty people present. Sixty others had been present in the morning to meet them, but were obliged to return to their homes before night.

The missionaries took a small tent with them, which during the evening and ensuing morning was filled by the Sikhs. Some even brought their wives and daughters to listen.

Late in the evening Mr. H. had them all sit down on the rug of the tent in a circle, while he read and explained a portion of one of the Gospels. When he afterward knelt to pray they all of their own accord knelt with him, and, to his surprise, repeated every petition he uttered. There are very few among them who are able to read, and so many expressed a desire to learn that we could but lament our inability to open a school among them at present.

Soon after Mr. Humphrey's return from the Sikh village he laid his dak for Bareilly, where he was to meet the superintendent, now Dr. Butler, and see what could be done toward securing a house there for mission premises.

Before he left we all removed to the house we had rented in Moradabad, although it was scarcely habitable. There was neither a glass window nor door in the house, and we were therefore obliged to keep some of the doors open in order to see. The owner commenced repairing at once, however, and the house soon began to have a more comfortable appearance; but it was after all an unpleasant building, rife with bloody legends of the mutiny.

Mr. H. found that a large mansion could be obtained in Bareilly for our mission. It was situated two miles west of the city, while the English cantonment is on the other side. It is too far from the city to be a suitable site for our mission premises, neither do we fancy living so far from the cantonment while the frightful tragedies of 1857 are yet fresh in our memories; but there was no alternative, as it was the only available house at that time. So it was settled that Cashmere kotee should be rented a year at least.

Mr. Humphrey returned to Moradabad, and

in a few days started off our few goods to Bareilly accompanied by the servants we had engaged in Moradabad. Foremost among them was a native Christian man, Masih Baksh by name, whom we were so fortunate as to secure for house bearer. We also engaged a khansamah, a tall, fine-looking, heavily-bearded Mussulman, who rejoices in the name of Peer Buksh, and we consider him really a peer among his fellows.

We left Moradabad ourselves the evening of the twenty-fifth of February, and early next morning reached Cashmere Kotee. It stands in the center of a large plat of ground, surrounded by a ditch and tall Indian grass. On three sides are entrances, marked by high plastered brick pillars.

The Kotee has a foundation wall ten feet in depth, filled in with earth under the main building, but finished off in store-rooms under the verandah. The body of the building is fifty feet long and seventy-five wide, including deep verandahs both in the front and rear, from which broad stairs descend to the ground.

On either side are wings of nearly the same width as the main part, and thirty feet in length. There are no chambers. The roof is flat, and we find it an agreeable place to sit at evening whenever we can muster strength enough to climb the stairs. That these are tiresome you will believe when I tell you that the rooms are twenty-five feet in height. We cannot have paper on our walls on account of the white ants; but we color them light green, blue, straw color, etc.

There are also fine cornices in each room, and very pretty mouldings around the doors and fireplaces. There are glass folding-doors placed directly opposite each other, so that the house can be aired quickly and thoroughly; but there are no windows, except in the dressing and bath rooms.

The house was not in very good condition when we entered it. The mutiny had left its traces even here. The buildings were defaced, glass broken, and walls blackened; but under the transforming power of mortar and white-wash, together with the handicraft of native masons, something of the original state of things is regained.

The garden attached to Cashmere Kotee is even now very beautiful. It is surrounded by a double row of hedge, between which we often walk and drive, and is laid out in walks and beds, interspersed with fruit trees. There are two varieties of the peach, two of the mango, guavas, custard apples, and several inferior kinds of fruit indigenous to the country.

We have an excellent moonshee living with us. His name is Azim Ali. He was a member of the band of native Christians that was gathered in Futteghur, and with them endured persecutions during the mutiny. His wife is a former pupil of Mrs. Poorie's school in Calcutta.

We have also a Eurasian preacher and his family with us. His name is Joseph Fieldbrave. His wife Sophia is an intelligent Christian woman. Rose Anna, the eldest child, is a pretty, bright little girl nine years of age. Isaac, the son, is a year or two younger, and the third is a babe.

We are much interested in these natives of India who bear the name of Christ, especially as this is our first mission station, and these our first associates in the missionary work.

The Hindoos celebrated the last days of February and the three first of March as the Holee festival. Its origin is said to be on this wise. A certain man had a sister who was a monster and killer of children, and who troubled many people. He also had a son whose name was Prahlad. This son was a worshiper of Ram, but the father was this god's greatest adversary, and was highly displeased at his son's devotion. His sister, Doonda, the monster, said to him one day, "You make a pile of wood and I will take Prahlad in my lap and sit on the pile; when I am seated you must set fire to the pile; I will escape and Prahlad will be destroyed." The plan was carried out, but, contrary to her expectations, she was consumed and Prahlad was saved, doubtless through the aid of Ram. Ever since this event the people have held this festival in its commemoration.

Upon the great day of the festival they have pooja in the morning and make bonfires at midnight. At this hour they march round their fires seven times with ears of barley-corn in their hands, which they afterward throw into the fire. The next day they throw a red powder over each other, and have great feasting and rejoicing. Friends visit each other and exchange congratulations that they are all alive to witness another Holee festival.

The Ram-Numee festival was held the last of March, in commemoration of the birth of Ram, who is the seventh incarnation of Vishnoo. This god became incarnate in order to destroy the monster Rawan, the king of Ceylon, which he effected by the help of Hanooman, the head of the apes. On this day the Hindoos fast, and repair to their temples, beat drums, and sing the praises of Ram. They also bathe his image with a mixture of both sweet and sour milk, butter, sugar, and honey. At midday they burn incense, and offer it flowers and food!

LETTER X.

Acquaintances in Bareilly — Orphan Boys and the Tiger — Effect produced by Bazar Preaching — School — Inquirers — Rumors in regard to the Mission — Zahoor-ul-Haqq — Hot Season — Dust Storm — Fruit.

BAREILLY, June 1, 1859.

MY DEAR MOTHER,—Among the first to welcome us to Bareilly were Mr. Ross, chaplain of the Forty-second Highlanders, Mr. Cowie, the civil chaplain, Capt. and Mrs. Unwin, Lieut. and Mrs. Hoggan. The Commissioner of Rohilcund also, and several other civil and military officers, have called and expressed an interest in our work.

We have indeed been agreeably surprised by the feeling manifested among Europeans in the cause of missions. The experience of 1857 has not been in vain. It is now realized, somewhat, that the only sure foundation on which English power in India can rest is the Christian religion. The time for forbidding missionaries to preach and teach the Gospel is past, and native Christians are no longer cast out from government employ, but are preferred instead.

The Commissioner has subscribed five hundred rupees to our general mission fund, and others have aided us liberally.

Here is the copy of a note received from the principal of the Bareilly Government College, which has been lately reorganized. I presume it is a fair exponent of the views of our English friends as to what sort of people missionaries should be.

MY DEAR SIR,—I have much pleasure in sending you rupees one hundred. I appreciate the character of an honest Christian missionary as one of the noblest on earth, and am desirous to support his efforts; and I am of opinion that as long as he is honest and simple-minded, and keeps himself "unspotted from the world," (impure as is our Anglo-Indian world,) that the natives will appreciate him too.

Wishing you Godspeed, I remain yours, etc.,

M. KEMPSON.

Bareilly is situated about sixty miles southeast from Moradabad, near the Ramgunga river, which is a tributary of the Gunga or Ganges. The main bazar is over two miles in length. It is now undergoing extensive repairs under the direction of the English magistrate. The shops have similar fronts of hard plaster in mouldings and flowers, which are very pretty and unique. At intervals there are beautifully ornamented gateways arching over the streets. Furniture of superior finish and quality is manufactured

9

in Bareilly; also jewelry, vessels of copper, brass, etc. The population is about 100,000.

We received a visit one day from three Hindoo gentlemen, with one of whom, Girdhara Sing, we were previously acquainted. They sat some time conversing with Mr. H., until he was called from the room. When he had left, one of the gentlemen said hurriedly to Girdhara Sing, "Ask the mem sahib." Girdhara turned to me and said, "Mem sahib, I cannot make my friends believe that you and the sahib never drink wine and brandy except as a medicine: I know you don't, for your servants told me so, but my friends think an Englishman could not live without their daily use." I said to them, "We certainly do not use them except as medicines."

"Does your religion," they asked, "prohibit their use."

I answered, "We think that the word of God, which is our guide, does prohibit the intemperate use of any blessings we have, and many people cannot use wines temperately; if they taste them they drink so much as to ruin themselves, soul and body; and as we are also taught to be watchful over each other, to bear the infirmities of the weak, etc., we think it is our duty to refrain from these intoxicating beverages, so that our influence may not make others to offend, but keep them from sin instead."

Just then Mr. H. came in and added, "We find that wines do us more good as medicines than they would if we used them daily."

"Doubtless it is so, sahib," they answered, and turning to Girdhara Sing remarked, "we are convinced."

Soon after our arrival we dispatched Masih Buksh to Nynee Tal to fetch the three orphan boys still remaining there, James Gowan having gone to Lucknow. When coming down the hill they were attacked by a tiger, but through Masih Buksh's courage and presence of mind escaped without injury.

Mr. Humphrey and his two helpers commenced preaching regularly in the city as soon as we became settled, and there was always an eager, and sometimes an angry multitude to listen.

The city was surveyed and a regular plan of appointments made out; Monday at such a well, Tuesday at such a bazar, etc. Wells seemed to be the favorite pulpits, as people gather about them at eventide; and as they come to draw water, the preachers tell them, as did the compassionate Saviour, of the water of life, "of which if a man drink he shall never thirst."

The Mussulmans were furious at this invasion of their faith; the Hindoos quite as much so, but a little quieter in their demonstrations.

One evening a Mussulman said to Mr. Humphrey while preaching, "O yes, you can say what you like now, sahib, for it is your reign; but if it were ours we'd put a stop to such talk very quickly," and his eyes glittered with malice.

"We don't doubt that in the least," replied Mr. H. "You have just shown us by your fiendish cruelty during the mutiny what you would do if you could; but it is our reign now, and why? Because the Christian religion is to be spread everywhere, and since you will not allow it to be preached under your rule, God has placed the British power in authority over this land."

Weeks passed on. We organized a school in a spare room of the kotee composed of our three orphan boys, Joseph's boy and girl, Masih Baksh, and two young men who came to us from the Sikh villages south of Moradabad.

These last were twin brothers, Minepul and Gurdial Sing. They seemed from the first acquaintance we had with them to be much impressed by the truth, and after the spring harvest had passed (for they were farmers) they left their home, journeyed eighty miles to us, and begged permission to work sufficiently to pay for their food, and to be allowed to give the rest of their time to study.

They wished to learn to read the word of

God for themselves, and to find the way of life, and walk in it. They proved to be industrious and singularly free from guile, and are making good although slow progress in knowledge.

Several men from the city have come to us as inquirers; but after long conversations with them we ascertained that their chief anxiety was to obtain recommendations to the civil officers, that they might obtain government employ; accordingly we dismissed them with the assurance that we could not recommend them to the magistrates and judges, as we were in no way connected with government. Our only object was to lead them to the true God.

The natives are slow to comprehend disinterestedness, as they have so little in their own character; therefore they persist in saying that we are to be paid for our converts by government, so much per head. The report has been rife in Bareilly that we are to receive one thousand rupees ($500) apiece for all the Christians we make, and they suppose the process of making Christians to be a supernatural one, a kind of incantation.

These prejudices we must of course live down, and I think on this account, if for no other reason, our "only two years in a place" rule is not suited to India.

June 10, 1859.

One Sabbath morning, at our early service in the long central room of the kotee, I noticed a stranger. He was evidently a Mussulman and a scholar, and his keen eye and composed demeanor showed that he possessed more than an ordinary amount of intelligence and culture.

The thought came into my mind, "There is a conceited Mussulman come down from the city to hear the preaching, that he may controvert it afterward." After service I remarked something of the kind to Mr. H., but he replied earnestly, "No, he did not come to provoke controversy, but to inquire into the truth;" and added that he believed him to be an intelligent and sincere inquirer.

Zahoor-ul-Haqq, for that was his name, came to us daily throughout that week, and at its close evinced a strong determination to identify himself with us as a Christian believer. He asked no favors, needed none, as he was in the service of some Mohammedan gentlemen as a teacher of their sons, and thus earned a comfortable livelihood; but he had felt uneasy in regard to his prospect for eternity for a long time. He felt that the Mohammedan creed was not sufficient for his need, and he believed that he recognized in the Christian religion a fitness to the wants of man that spoke its origin divine. He therefore asked Mr. H. to baptize him on the ensuing Sabbath. But Mr. Humphrey thought best to have him wait a week, and said to him, "I should very much dislike to baptize you before you are fully decided, as it would have an injurious effect upon others should you afterward return to Mohammedanism, so we will wait one week, and if at its close you still desire it I will receive you into the Church of God by baptism."

Zahoor-ul-Haqq acquiesced pleasantly, although he was evidently disappointed. He remarked, "You'll find me of the same mind next Sabbath."

We then held our usual morning service, and afterward the Sabbath-school. Mr. H. explained the eighth chapter of Mark to the native preachers, Masih Baksh, Zahoor-ul-Haqq, and others. After reading that verse, "What shall it profit a man if he gain the whole world and lose his own soul," etc., Mr. H. remarked on this wise: "When a man dies his soul enters upon a new sphere; none of the accompaniments of this life can be taken with him, therefore all he has gathered here of this world's wealth will be of no use to him in that new state of existence. If he has fully believed on the Lord Jesus Christ, and manifested his belief by a good life, his soul will enter into the joys of heaven; but if he has not, if all his energies have been employed in the acquisition of wealth, or any merely worldly object, his soul will be cast out of that happy place into darkness and banishment from the presence of God for evermore. He will lose his soul! What shall it profit him then that he possesses even the whole world?"

"Nothing," said the listeners simultaneously; and Zahoor-ul-Haqq added with energy, "Sahib, why not baptize me now? I may die before to-morrow without having manifested my belief in the Lord Jesus Christ."

He spoke so earnestly that we all started with surprise. Mr. H. replied, "Be patient till next Sabbath, and give your time meanwhile to prayer and the study of the Scriptures. God sees your willingness to honor him before men, and will as surely accept it as if really shown forth in deeds, should you die before an opportunity to do so is given you."

The question dropped, but our hearts were filled with joy at his intelligent earnestness in the matter.

During the week all the arts and influences possible were brought to bear upon Zahoor-ul-Haqq by his Mohammedan relatives. His father came more than thirty miles to see him, to beseech, threaten, or bribe, as he might find necessary. He tried the three methods in succession without the slightest effect, and in despair gave up his son to his dreadful infatuation. His wife sent him word that he should never live with her more, nor ever have possession of his two children if he forsook the faith of Mohammed;

but when the Sabbath dawned Zahoor-ul-Haqq was ready and waiting for the simple ceremony that typifies so marvelous a change in man—the deliberate turning from error to truth, from darkness to light, from Satan to God.

I have seen scores in our own land take the vows of Christ upon them by baptism, and have always regarded the sight as one of the most beautiful which earth can afford, causing saints and angels to rejoice with great joy; but I never realized the full import of that precious sacrament as I did that lovely Sabbath morning when this first convert in our mission renounced the faith of the false prophet for that of the Son of God.

Zahoor-ul-Haqq's daily life since that time has been all we could wish. We have engaged him as a teacher in our school at the same salary he was receiving in the city. We disliked to set the precedent, but our need was urgent, as Azim Ali and his wife have been removed to Moradabad.

The hot wind is now having full sway over these plains. It commenced the first of April, and has blown regularly ever since. It rises daily about eight o'clock A. M., and falls about five in the evening. We keep the doors closely shut during the intervening hours and the punkahs swinging, and strive to forget our lassitude and discomfort in study.

The school is held in the early morning. It has been increased lately by the arrival of two more Sikhs and one more orphan; the latter was sent us by the magistrate.

Our bazar preaching is held at evening, and all the livelong day we remain shut up in this large cool mansion. Cool, did I say? I fancy you would not call it so were you to step inside it just now, as the punkah-walla, that is, the man who pulls the punkah, has just managed to break the slender bamboo to which the punkah rope is attached, and while he is fastening on a new one the atmosphere of the room relapses into a dead heat.

We have had several terrific dust-storms lately. During one of them the darkness was so intense that we were obliged to light candles at mid-day; but the "chota barsat," or little rainy season, is close at hand, and then we shall probably have some relief from this intense heat.

We have now an abundance of fruit, mangoes and peaches, guavas, etc.; but we are obliged to exercise great caution in regard to eating fruit of any kind.

The mango is a large oval-shaped fruit, of a green color; but when fully ripe slightly tinged with yellow. Beneath the rind is a soft pulpy substance of a bright orange color, and very delicious flavor. The guavas resemble large pears in appearance. Their taste is pleasant; but we do not eat them unless cooked, as they are said to be hurtful.

We have both suffered in health somewhat of course, but our English friends and physician say that we bear the heat very well indeed. I think our lonely situation helps to make us low-spirited at times, as well as the heat; but as we are pioneers in this part of the great field we must bear this patiently. I hope, however, that the time will be brief, as we hear that a large party of missionaries sailed from Boston in April for India. May God protect them on the great deep and bring them safely to us. We regret that they sailed so early in the year, as they will be obliged to come up the country in August, and we fear some among them may not be strong enough to bear the fatigue of traveling in such oppressive weather as we are sure to have during that month.

But I must close; and just now as I think of the long journey these pages will make, my mind's eye glances at their destination, the white farm-house in old St. Lawrence, where my mother and my brothers dwell, and I long to open wide the door that I may catch a glimpse of the familiar forms within. I see the blooming garden, and the waving grass of the meadow just beyond; but hark! what dissonant voice is that: "Khana taiyar hai," (dinner is ready,) and my beautiful mirage vanishes, and in its stead is my matted floor, the high bare walls, the swinging punkah, and the dusky form in the doorway with a hand gracefully waving toward the waiting dinner, so I must bid adieu to day-dreams for the present.

Mission Premises at Bareilly.

LETTER XI.

Rainy Season — Its Accompaniments — Beetles — Reptiles, etc. — Masih Buksh — Arrival of Missionaries — Journey to Lucknow — Items in regard to the City — Annual Meeting No. 1 — Return to Bareilly — Death of Mr. Downey.

BAREILLY, *September* 25, 1859.

MY DEAR MOTHER,—On the fifteenth day of June

> "God sent his messenger the rain,
> And said unto the mountain brook,
> 'Rise up, and from thy caverns look,
> And leap with naked snow-white feet
> From the cool hills into the heat
> Of the broad arid plain."

Never did we give rain such a welcome as then. It poured, it sparkled, it bubbled, and O how both vegetable and animal life were refreshed! The hot wind was banished, and a delicious coolness pervaded the atmosphere; but after a few days the rain ceased, and for a week the weather was hot and close. The sun poured its heat upon the saturated ground, and a steamy, malarious atmosphere was the consequence. Then the burra barsat (big rainy season) set in, and we had alternate rain and sunshine for two and a half months.

On the whole we found the rainy season more

trying than the hot, as the sudden changes occasioned chills and colds. The ground and air became alive with reptiles and insects; serpents, centipedes, scorpions, toads, lizards, and worms on the ground, and every imaginable kind of beetle and butterfly in the air and in the houses. The cobra-capello, or hooded snake, is very common. An officer in Bareilly found one in his sleeping-room soon after the rains commenced, and had some difficulty in dispatching him. It is no unusual thing to find a scorpion on the wall, or behind a door, or even in a shoe. But the reptile most dreaded by the natives is the large black snake. I knew of three deaths resulting from their bite last season.

The seventeenth of August is observed by Hindoos as a day of prayer to be preserved from the bites of serpents. Religious (?) ceremonies are performed, and a certain great serpent is worshiped.

We have lost Masih Buksh, our Christian bearer. His wife's father, who is in a Roman Catholic mission near Meerut, has succeeded in getting his services for a while. He went only to keep peace with his wife, and will come back to our mission as soon as possible. I do not think there is any fear of his becoming a Romanist. We have Minepul Sing as house-bearer now, and he really does very well.

During the last days of August we heard of

several cases of fever and cholera in the city, but were mercifully spared all serious illness ourselves.

We rejoiced greatly when we heard of the safe arrival of our missionaries. The reinforcement consisted of Mr. and Mrs. Baume and their little son, Mr. and Mrs. Parker, Mr. and Mrs. Judd, Mr. and Mrs. Waugh, Mr. and Mrs. Downey, and Mr. Thoburn. We were only waiting their arrival to hold our first annual meeting in Lucknow, so we left Bareilly about the time they left Calcutta in order to have a little visit in Lucknow before their arrival. As we traveled in palkees, and Mr. Knowles and Mr. Parsons were in company with us, we formed quite a procession. All the long night and till near the succeeding midday we endured the shaking of the palkees.

We should have arrived in Futteghur in the morning had the Ganges been in its normal state; but it was much swollen from the recent rains, and the rude boats that took us across were almost unmanageable. The heat was intense, and it seemed to us that we were baked to the full extent of endurance; but when we were set down by the cool-looking dak bungalow in Futteghur our spirits came to us again, and we sang out with some energy, considering our recent feeble condition, for the khansamah, and ordered refreshments.

We went on in the evening by horse dak. The horses had changed for the better since our memorable ride in 1858, but still the journey was very fatiguing. I look back and wonder that I dared to make that trip at that season of the year; but I was famishing for society, and thought the joy of meeting our friends would compensate for the fatigues of the journey, and so it did a hundredfold.

We reached Cawnpore about ten o'clock A. M., rested three or four hours, and then hastened on to Lucknow, where we arrived about nine o'clock in the evening. I shall not soon forget the welcome we received there, and the delightful visit we enjoyed with our friends.

We were glad to find Jóel and his family (which had joined him in Lucknow) well and happy, also James Gowan and several orphan girls looking happy, and evidently making progress in the right way.

We spent Saturday and Monday in driving about the ancient and once regal city of Lucknow. We saw the fort, the splendid Imambarah, a moslem cathedral, the yet beautiful temples, the still magnificent palaces; but from them the glory has departed.

No wonder the native nobles mourn the decay of so much grandeur. One of the king's palaces is now occupied by missionaries of the

Church of England. We saw the gateway where the gallant Neill fell, and the battered and frowning residency, now so well known as the scene of the fearful siege of 1857, and where the noble Sir Henry Lawrence died.

Lucknow extends about four miles along the bank of the river Goomtee. Aside from the numerous palaces and temples, the buildings are very wretched. The city is now undergoing extensive repairs and changes. Many of the huts have been leveled, and the streets widened. The population in 1853 was three hundred thousand.

Monday evening we all met in Dr. Butler's parlor to await the arrival of our friends. They came at last, and O what a meeting it was! Probably never again will missionaries be received among us with such joy, because never again will circumstances be the same. The mutiny, and our consequent discouragements and dangers, our long and lonely waiting, all had wrought up our feelings to an unusual pitch. They were all in pretty good health, except Mr. and Mrs. Downey, who seemed to have suffered much from exposure to the heat.

Our first annual meeting commenced next day in the newly-finished mission chapel; and continued till the Wednesday of the succeeding week. The appointments were as follows:

Lucknow, Rev. R. PIERCE, J. CAWDELL.
Shahjehanpore, Rev. J. W. WAUGH.
Bareilly, Rev. J. L. HUMPHREY, Rev. J. B. DOWNEY.
Moradabad, Rev. C. W. JUDD, J. PARSONS.
Bijnour, Rev. E. W. PARKER.
Nynee Tal, Rev. J. M. THOBURN, S. KNOWLES.

You notice one other name in the list besides the missionaries with whom I have made you acquainted. Mr. Cawdell came out to Calcutta as a Bible reader, I believe. He has joined our mission at Lucknow quite recently.

A boys' orphanage was located at Bareilly, and one for orphan girls in Lucknow, Mr. Downey to have charge of the boys, and Mrs. Pierce of the girls.

During the last days of the meeting Mr. and Mrs. Downey were both ill, and had the advice of a physician. On the day it closed Mrs. Downey was better, but he seemed worse, although we did not anticipate a fatal termination to his illness. We hoped soon to welcome them both to Bareilly.

Wednesday evening Mr. and Mrs. Judd and ourselves bade our Lucknow friends good-by and commenced our homeward journey. They were to spend a fortnight with us, as the mission house at Moradabad (a recent purchase) was not yet vacated. Mr. and Mrs. Parker remained a while in Lucknow, as they were somewhat indisposed.

We had a more trying journey home than when we went to Lucknow, if that were possible. On Saturday, instead of reaching home by ten o'clock A. M., as we expected, we were exposed to the heat all the livelong day on the long dak from Futteghur to Bareilly. Twenty-two hours we lay in our palkees, only leaving them once for the purpose of procuring refreshments, in which undertaking we entirely failed.

About eight o'clock Saturday evening Cashmere Kotee again blessed our vision. Our native Christians and servants were on the look-out, and gave us a hearty welcome. We were so thoroughly fatigued that we kept our beds nearly all the next day, merely exerting ourselves to go out to our meals, and to hold one service in Hindoostanee.

The week succeeding we devoted ourselves to showing up the place, country, and people round about to Mr. and Mrs. Judd, not forgetting sundry reading lessons in Hindoostanee.

One morning we went by invitation to breakfast with some of our English friends, and while at their house we received a letter from Lucknow informing us that Mr. Downey was dead. It was a great blow to us. We could scarcely believe it possible that he was indeed thus cut down on the very threshold of the missionary work. He was so amiable and talented that we had formed high expectations of his future usefulness.

A letter from Sister Pierce, written a few days after his death, reads as follows:

"Brother Downey was buried last Saturday evening in our little cemetery, where his body will await the resurrection, while his glorified spirit is rejoicing in the light of God's countenance. He has truly given himself for India. O that this death may accomplish more for this unhappy people than his life would have done!

"Dear Sister Downey exhibits in a wonderful manner the sustaining influences of grace. I remained with her during the night after his burial, and I shall never forget it. She said at one time, 'O how desolate I am, and yet how my comforts abound!' She will go to Bareilly, and as far as she can will do the work Brother Downey would have done. She told him when he was dying, 'My own love, God being my helper, I will live and die for India, and the people for whom you have prayed so much.' She will go to Bareilly in company with Brother and Sister Parker, who expect to leave soon for Bijnour."

Three Hindoo holidays occur in the month of September. One is in remembrance of the fifth incarnation of Vishnoo to prevent the king Balee from obtaining dominion over the three worlds—heaven, earth, and the region below the earth. Another is in honor of the birth of Janesh, the god of learning and prudence. This god is invoked by all students and authors before they commence their respective labors. On the third holiday "pooja" is performed for the benefit of the souls of departed ancestors, among whom they reckon crows! This notion is in accordance with their theory of the transmigration of souls, which is an important part of the Hindoo religion. According to their belief, heaven consists in a soul being absorbed in the divine nature, just as a river becomes one with the ocean by falling into it. Hell consists in a soul being sent into the body of a very inferior animal.

The weather is growing decidedly cooler, although still very oppressive. Custard apples are ripe now, and are very delicious as well as wholesome. They are about the size of an ordinary apple, and are covered with a thick scaly rind. The pulp is white and sweet, something like custard, hence its name.

We are feeling stronger since the rains entirely ceased, and hope to be able to itinerate among the villages in the district of Barielly in a few weeks.

LETTER XII.

Visit with Friends — Arrival of Mrs. Downey — Hindoo Festival — Arrival of Dr. Butler and Family — Commence Itinerating — A Peep behind the Purdah — Journey to Budaon — Lieut. Governor — Nawab of Rampore — Robbery — Budaon to be a Mission Station—Baptisms—Removal.

BUDAON, Jan. 30, 1860.

MY DEAR MOTHER,—Mr. and Mrs. Parker, with Mrs. Downey, came to Bareilly the first of October. On the evening after their arrival Mr. and Mrs. Judd left us for Moradabad. Mrs. Downey bears her great sorrow with meekness and resignation, but her grief preys upon her spirits and health. She calls forth our tenderest sympathy. Mr. Downey was to have charge of the boy's orphanage, and it is thought best for Mrs. Downey to occupy that position now.

Thomas Cullen, a native Christian catechist, is to assist her, and there are several teachers and servants, so that we trust the care will not be too much for her to undertake.

Mr. and Mrs. Parker remained with us a fortnight, and we enjoyed many walks and drives together in the country round about.

There is a beautiful garden, owned by a wealthy Hindoo gentleman, very near us, and our friends were charmed with it as well as with our own more unpretending grounds. Just outside this garden a great annual jubilee was held on the twentieth of October, in commemoration of the victóry of Ram over Rawan, the ten-headed monster and King of Ceylon.

An immense figure of wicker work was raised and filled with fireworks. This was the effigy of the King of Ceylon. A fine looking Hindoo lad, on a gayly caparisoned elephant, represented Ram.

An immense concourse of people, all arrayed in bright colors, assembled to witness the destruction of the figure. A confused clangor was kept up with great zeal on drums and odd-looking tin and brass instruments. At the appointed time the representative Ram set fire to the wicker monster, which, amid the frantic cheers of the multitude, exploded, and blazed away till it was consumed.

Soon after Mr. and Mrs. Parker left, Dr. Butler and family arrived from Lucknow, together with the orphan boys that had been gathered in that place.

As soon as the orphanage was made over to Mrs. Downey, and we were free from the care of the school, we thought best to commence itinerating, a course that is generally pursued by missionaries in the cold season. We started in primitive style. A bullock cart was loaded with a tent, table, bed, chairs, cooking utensils, and a box of provisions, and with two or three servants was sent in advance. Mr. H. and I made our march of ten miles on horseback.

We stopped at midday and ate our luncheon under a wide-spreading mango tree in the midst of a fine grove or "tope." As we admired the luxuriant foliage of the trees we could but contrast it in our minds with the appearance of our trees at home at that season of the year.

Our trees here are never leafless. All the year round their thickly-clothed branches give welcome shade to man and beast, but during the spring months leaves are falling continually and new ones shooting forth, until the whole mass of foliage is silently and almost imperceptibly renewed. The natives use the dry leaves for fuel.

The road was so terribly "kutchah" that when we arrived at Futtegunge, the village where we were to encamp, we found our cart had but just arrived. A site was selected in a grove just outside the village, the tent was soon put up, and we commenced tentkeeping.

We staid there several days. Joseph was with us, and accompanied Mr. H. in his frequent trips to the village to preach to the people, to converse with them and give them books. Numbers came to our tents asking for books and tracts, and all appeared to be curious and interested.

I went one evening into the village and entered the courtyard of a Mohammedan family. The family dwellings were around it on three sides, and the women of the household, twenty or twenty-five in number, being the daughters, daughters-in-law, and granddaughters of the heads of the family, were scattered over the yard, spinning cotton, cleaning brass cups and plates, taking care of babies, etc., etc. They gathered round me with great apparent interest, gave me a comfortable morha (cane stool) to sit on, and overwhelmed me with questions.

When they ascertained that my husband was neither a magistrate nor judge, colonel nor captain, but a padre sahib instead, they asked why we had come out to their village. I explained that he is a different padre sahib from the chaplains, that we were not from Europe but from the new world, "America des see," and that we came to teach the Hindoostanee people about the true God, and how they might obtain forgiveness for their sins, and secure everlasting life and happiness. They asked many questions, which I answered as best I could, and when I left they urged me to come again.

The succeeding night considerable rain fell, and our tent was flooded. We made an inglorious retreat next morning to Cashmere Kotee, as the weather was changeable and our tent was not a good one. The exposure brought on an attack of neuralgia, which obliged me to remain at home for a fortnight, and Mr. H. and Joseph had the itinerating all to themselves.

Zahoor-ul-Haqq accompanied Mr. H. on one trip, and one evening preached for the first time in a large village near Shahjehanpore. Mr. H. noticed that he appeared agitated at the time, and learned afterward that it was his native village!

Zahoor-ul-Haqq did not set himself to preaching. He is too modest for that. But his words in our social meetings were so well chosen, and were uttered in so convincing a manner, that we urged him to go forth and bear witness to the truth among the people. He bids fair to become a very useful preacher.

About the twelfth of December we started again in company, determined to have a long tour. This time we journeyed in a covered two-wheeled vehicle called a shigram, drawn by oxen. We were bound for Budaon, a city about twenty-eight miles from Bareilly in a southerly direction.

We were two nights on the road. Mr. H. and Joseph preached in several villages as we went along, and distributed tracts and gospels to all who could read.

We reached Budaon on the evening of the third day, and pitched our tents (we had two) on an open space a little out from the city, near the European residences. Before we were settled two natives came and welcomed us to Budaon, saying they were Christians and had long been praying that missionaries might come into the place. We had heard of them previously, and knew something of their history. They were members of a small society of native Christians that was formed in Bareilly before the mutiny by a zealous chaplain of the Church of England.

I say native Christians, although it is probable that very few of them know anything of a change of heart. They have, however, been baptized and initiated into the use of the Prayer Book. A school has been kept up among them most of the time, and they are therefore far in advance of their heathen neighbors in intelligence.

Three brothers from this little band, with their families, had removed to Budaon previous to the mutiny, and procured government employ. When the Sepoy regiment stationed at that place mutinied they fled to an obscure village, where they remained unmolested until Budaon was reoccupied by the English, when they immediately returned.

We arranged our tents comfortably, and concluded to make something of a stay in Budaon. Mr. H. and Joseph preached often in the city to multitudes of eager listeners, and could scarcely supply the demand for tracts and gospels.

The native Christians urged us to commence a mission in the place at once, and pointed out an unfinished kotee nearly opposite our camping ground, which was for sale, and would make a suitable mission house.

Mr. H. wrote to Dr. Butler a report of our reception, and the favorable opinion we had formed of the place, and asked him to join us if he should judge best to entertain the project of commencing a mission there immediately. In a day or two he arrived, and was so well pleased with the prospect at Budaon, that he concluded to purchase the kotee and have us remove there as soon as possible.

About this time Mr. Edmonstone, the Lieutenant-governor of the Northwest Provinces, with his suite, arrived in the place on his usual winter tour, and encamped a short distance from us. Their tents were arranged in streets, and formed quite a little village.

The nawab of Rampore also, who since his staunch championship during the mutiny is quite a favorite with the government, came to Budaon to meet the lieutenant-governor, and his large and irregular cluster of tents was resplendent with barbaric finery.

On the twenty-fourth of December we received tickets of invitation to a Christmas dinner to be given at the lieutenant-governor's tent the next evening. We retired to rest later than usual that night, as Dr. Butler and Mr. H. were busy looking about the city until evening. We noticed an unusual number of natives lurking about, but did not take any more precautions than usual. Our bullocks were fastened near the tents, and their drivers slept in the carts near them. Our servants slept under a tree near the tents, and one lay across the main entrance to our tent.

It is the custom in India to have a watchman, a chowkeedar as he is called, to keep watch throughout the night whenever a house is out of military cantonment, and when itinerating, on account of the great number of robbers in the country. But we had never had one when itinerating, and had never been disturbed in any way. Upon that night we did not even take the precaution to keep a lamp burning.

We slept quietly until about four o'clock in the morning, just that darkest time that precedes the dawn, when I was wakened by a clicking sound. I listened, and distinctly heard a noise as if a dog ran across the tent just beyond the head of our bed. I waked Mr. H. and asked him to light the lamp quickly, as I thought there were dogs in the tent, a not unusual thing by the way. He struck a light and looked around the tent, but saw nothing unusual. I then glanced around and saw that our two trunks were missing.

"Our trunks!" I exclaimed, "where are they?"

"Where, sure enough!" said Mr. H., and just then we saw the tent was open on either side in a line with the place where the trunks had stood.

"There have been robbers here," we said simultaneously, and we awakened our servants at once, and dressed quickly as possible. Peer Buksh and the other servants came in directly. We told them what had occurred, and giving them a lantern sent them off to chase the robbers, while Mr. A. should call the police. Before he had started, however, a servant came running back with the intelligence that they could discern the robbers making off across the fields toward a grove.

There was a grand chase for a while, and then the robbers seeing they would soon be overtaken, stopped, opened the trunks, and turned everything out upon the ground. They then sought and took what money happened to be there, (only about sixteen dollars,) tore off the brass clasps from a memorandum book, and last, but not least, my broche shawl, and ran away, leaving everything else strewed on the grass.

Christmas evening we dined at the lieutenant-governor's tent. His suite, and all the English residents of the station, were present. These last were not many, only three families.

Mr. Edmonstone is a fine-looking gentleman, apparently about fifty years of age. The officers of his suite were quite social and agreeable, and so were the ladies and gentlemen of the station. I noticed that the gentlemen drank wine quite freely, especially two or three of them, and were quite hilarious in consequence. After dinner a short time was spent in conversation, and the party broke up.

The next day we returned to Bareilly, and soon as the purchase of the house in Budaon was completed, made preparation to remove. The evening previous to our departure from Bareilly Mr. H. baptized Minepul Sing, Khan Sing, also a Sikh, and Hosain Buksh, a young man from Lucknow. Gurdial Sing, the brother of Minepul, had previously gone to Bijnour to Mr. Parker.

The fatigue consequent upon our removal was too much for me, and I have been ill ever since. I am but just beginning to study again, but there is so much confusion and discomfort on account of the work which is being done on the house that I find it a difficult matter to keep my attention fixed upon any subject. I hope, however, that this delightful cold season will so invigorate me that I shall soon recover my balance both of mental and physical strength.

We left Minepul Sing in Bareilly, as bearer for the Boys' Orphanage, and I miss him very much, as we have not been able to supply his place, and I have consequently been obliged to do many things for which I have not sufficient strength, and do not wish to spare the time, for I count every moment lost, aside from needful duties and recreation, that is not spent in the study of the language or in direct intercourse with the natives.

LETTER XIII.

Epitome of the Hindoo Religion — Natal, Marriage, and Funeral Ceremonies — Seasons — Products of the Country.

BUDAON, March 20, 1860.

MY DEAR MOTHER,—I received a letter from you a few weeks ago, in which you asked me to give you an epitome of the Hindoo articles of faith and an outline of their customs, etc. The reason I have not done so ere this is, that I have not known the one nor the other sufficiently well to do so, nor do I now except in theory. That theory has been furnished us in a very interesting little work entitled "Domestic Manners and Customs of the Hindoos of Northern India," by Baboo Ishuree Dass, a native Christian Catechist of Futteghur.

The most ancient of the Hindoo scriptures, according to him, teach the worship of one supreme being. In later times, when the people sunk into gross idolatry, other books were written called the "Veds." These inculcate the worship of gods, goddesses, images, animals, rivers, and almost everything a Hindoo likes or fears.

According to these later scriptures, the deity

has resolved himself into three forms, called Brahma, Vishnoo, and Mahesh. The work of the first is creation, of the second preservation, and of the third, destruction. A female principal is joined to each, called respectively Saraswatee, Lakshmee, and Doorga or Devee. Brahma, the first person of this triad, was cursed by a god on account of his sins, and his worship ceased throughout the country long ago. According to their Veds, Vishnoo and Mahesh, or Shiva, as he is called sometimes, have been guilty of great sins too; but the Hindoos, with characteristic inconsistency, continue to worship them.

The worshipers of Vishnoo are more numerous than those of Mahesh. They believe he became incarnate several times, and in several different forms. He became a fish to fetch up the four Veds, or principal scriptures, from the ocean in which they had been lost; a tortoise to support the earth during a deluge; once he took the form of a lion to kill a man; and again he became incarnate, by the name of Ram, to kill the King of Ceylon. The last time he will come, the Hindoos say, to punish all the wicked.

Besides these two persons of the Hindoo triad, their wives, and incarnations, there are thousands of other gods, goddesses, and various objects of worship. The sun, moon, stars, heroes, mountains, rivers, trees, beasts, and reptiles are their gods. Even pens and instands are worshiped at certain times; because, as they say, they obtain knowledge by them.

Bathing is one of the most important duties Hindoos have to perform. Without it, they will neither eat nor worship.

At the time of bathing they worship the sun, by offering it water in both hands and addressing it with prayers. There is a peculiar prayer which every strict Hindoo is bound to repeat three times a day. There is one for each of the four general castes, but that which is for the Brahmins is said to be the most efficacious. It is considered very sacred; and a Brahmin will never repeat it before people of a lower caste. This prayer is said to procure the forgiveness of all sins and to make the heart perfectly holy.

The following is a translation: "O earth, firmament, and heaven, we meditate on the great light of the sun; may it enlighten our hearts." It has one merit at least, that of brevity.

The worship of the gods through their representative idols is performed on this wise. The image, which is usually either of stone, brass, or clay, is set before them on a stand, when water is poured over it, that the god may be bathed as well as the worshipers. They then make marks on its forehead with a sweet smelling colored wood, and also on their own foreheads and chests. They then place fragrant leaves and flowers before the image, and burn incense before it in a little brass cup. The incense is composed of the sweet smelling wood before mentioned and one or two other kinds, also camphor and butter. They then light a lamp and move it in a circular way three or four times before the image; then present it offerings of sweatmeats, fruits, rice, etc. Before these offerings and the image they draw a curtain for a few moments, that the god may eat without embarrassment. Meanwhile a little bell is tinkling, and the people repeat hymns and count beads.

After the worship, or "pooja," is over, the image is removed and put in a safe place, and the offerings (all that the god did not eat) are eaten by the officiating priests and their families.

In the temples the idols are usually larger and stationary. Many, especially women, devote themselves to the worship of goddesses, especially that of Kalee and Doorga, or Devee, the wife of Shiva. The goddesses are said to be very bloodthirsty and cruel. In one of their Veds, Kalee is said to be pleased for a thousand years by a human sacrifice, and for one hundred thousand, if three human beings are offered her at once. Male buffaloes are sacrificed to Doorga, but she is far better pleased if a human head be offered her. Children were formerly kidnapped and sold for sacrifices. At the ordinary family pooja the women are not present, but hold service by themselves. On their holidays, however, and all extraordinary occasions, the women and children are mute observers.

The most marked feature of the Hindoo religion is caste. There are four principal castes: the Brahmins, or priests; the chutrees, or soldiers; vyshees, or merchants; and soodras. Each of these castes is subdivided into scores of others. Of the soodra caste are first the kyarths, or writers, then farmers, shoemakers, blacksmiths, and many others.

The Brahmins claim to be gods, and are so considered by others. People frequently prostrate themselves at their feet, and they receive their worship with the greatest complacency. Many of the Brahmins do not eat any animal food, and are very strict in the observance of religious duties. These are called "bhauts," or saints; others eat goat's flesh, fish, birds, etc.; but on no account would a Hindoo of any caste eat beef. They consider the cow to be a very sacred animal, and they will not even touch a piece of its flesh.

One of our missionaries was once reasoning with some Hindoos about their absurd notions in regard to the cow. "You drink her milk," said he, "and eat butter made from it; why, then, should you not eat her flesh?" A Brahmin replied with a sarcastic sneer, "You drank your mother's milk, but did you also eat her flesh?" You perceive these people are not wanting in shrewdness.

The different castes will by no means intermarry, nor even eat with each other. The distinction of caste is kept up with so great strictness that a man of low caste might be dying and one of a higher caste would not allow him to drink from his cup, as it would thereby be defiled.

According to the claims of caste the son is not at liberty to follow any trade or profession that he likes, but must adhere to that which his father and forefathers have practiced before him; doing otherwise would be followed by excommunication. This is the main reason why families are obliged to have so many servants. A man of the kahar caste will carry a palkee, dust furniture, brush clothing, carry letters, etc.; but he will not sweep the floors nor serve at tables, where, terrible to imagine, he might touch a plate that had beef on it. A dhobee also will wash and iron your clothing; but he will not do any other work.

The bheestees, or water-carriers, and the whole staff of table servants, are Mussulmans, who, although they have no caste, have nevertheless plenty of custom, "dustoor" they call it, which will not allow them to do anything but their regular work.

Mohammedans, you are aware, are as deadly enemies to pork as are the Jews; however, the bheestees fetch water to the houses in swine skins. These are neatly tanned and sewed up, and when filled with water and slung across the bheestees' backs, look marvelously like a new order of pigs.

In India the patriarchal system prevails in regard to families. When the daughters are married they go, of course, to live with their husbands; but when the sons marry they do not leave their father's house; they live with him, and continue under his direction and government. All the earnings of the sons are handed over to the father, and he provides for all the wants of the household, and has the general oversight and management of it.

The condition of females in India is truly pitiable. A Hindoo girl is never regarded as a member of her own father's family, but as belonging to that of her future husband, so that in reality she has no home until she has fulfilled her chief end in life, that is, until she is married. That event, however, occurs early in her history. Betrothal takes place usually when the children are both young, and when the girl is thirteen or fourteen years of age the "puckah" marriage is celebrated. The bridegroom is usually a few years older than the bride.

Of course where marriages are wholly planned

by the parents, without the interested parties having even seen each other, happiness in that relation is the exception instead of the rule. The wife, however, is bound to her husband by strong ties, as her happiness in this world and in a future state is based upon her obedience to him.

The Hindoo religion requires that if the husband die first the wife shall be burned with his corpse. In one of their sacred books is the following proverb: "As many hairs as are in the human body multiplied by a crore and a half crore,* so many years will she live in heaven who dies with her husband."

Although so very desirable a rite to Hindoo women, widow-burning, or "suttee," is prohibited by the British government, and Hindoo widows are now compelled to live on in a state of great unhappiness, not only because they cannot marry again, but because they are looked down upon with contempt, and have also the melancholy prospect of transmigrating into the body of some ill-favored bird or beast whenever they shall "shuffle off this mortal coil."

A Hindoo girl receives no mental culture. She cannot even read in her own language. Learning is not considered necessary for her, as she is not expected to be a companion to her husband. Her duty is merely to attend to house-

* A crore is equal to ten millions.

hold matters and sew on very plain garments. Most of the sewing, however, is done by men of the tailor caste.

The family washing, too, is usually given out to men of the dhobee caste, and as the houses are destitute of windows and nearly so of furniture, and as their food is extremely simple, Hindoo women are spared much of the toil which wears upon the wives and mothers of our own land.

Hindoos generally have but two meals a day, taking the first at mid-day. They pursue their various callings until eleven o'clock A. M., when they adjourn to a river, tank, or well, as the case may be, to perform their morning ablutions. They then have their pooja and their breakfast; and after a comfortable time with the native pipe, or hookah, they again go forth to their labors till the evening. Then they have dinner, another peaceful season with the hookah, and betake themselves to their simple bedstead. They have no beds, but merely a fine cording over their bedsteads and a blanket on it. They often sleep in the open air. The women do not eat with the male members of the family, but serve them first, and then have their own meals.

A Hindoo never mentions his wife by that term, nor by her name. He speaks of her if she have children, as the mother of the oldest son, as "Nundoo kee ma," that is, Nundoo's mother. If she have no children he simply says "she" or "my family." The wife likewise never mentions her husband's name, but speaks of him as the "child's father," or "he" or "mine."

I have mentioned the native dress in my previous letters, so that I need not say much on that subject. I will merely add that the women I have met in this section of country wear more ornaments than those I have formerly seen. Sometimes there is a ring entirely round the ear, from which clusters of pendants fall, quite concealing the entire ear. Their arms are often literally covered with bracelets. They wear rings in their noses varying in size from a dollar to the rim of a saucer; necklets, anklets, and toe-rings. On these last there are sometimes little bells, and the dusky wearers "make a tinkling as they go." Sometimes these ornaments are of gold and silver, but oftener they are of a white metal of inferior quality, and even of glass and tinsel.

Women sometimes smoke the hookah, but chewing "pawn" seems to be their grand resource against lassitude.

Pawn is put up in packages and sold in the market all ready for use, as regularly as rice or any article of food. It is composed of a piece of betelnut, cardamoms, cloves, and a little lime, all nicely wrapped in a pawnleaf and pinned together with a thorn. One of these suffices for the whole space between meals, and the use of it dyes the teeth a bright red, which is thought to be so becoming that the Hindoo women also dye their finger and toe-nails, the palms of their hands and the soles of their feet the same color.

In consequence of their utter lack of education, native women are necessarily frivolous, and childish in the extreme. Their tempers are ungovernable, and when angry they sometimes attempt to commit suicide.

I will now give you some description of their marriage, natal, and funeral ceremonies; but there are many meaningless rites not worth a full description.

According to the Hindoo Shasters (sacred writings) a girl is marriageable when she is seven years old. When parents wish their daughter to be married they call together their nearest relatives, and request them to select a boy for her from some desirable family.

The friends consult together and fix upon a boy. The family priest then procures the boy's horoscope and compares it with that of the girl, and if he considers the marriage will be an auspicious one he is sent with the family barber to the boy's house with presents, and if they are obliged to pay a certain sum, one fourth of the amount is also sent at that time. If the boy's parents are agreed they all perform "pooja" together, after which a mark is put upon the boy's forehead, and his father makes small presents to all in the house. This ceremony is called "teeka."

In a few days the priest of the bride's family makes out a paper, on which the days for the wedding ceremonies are written. A duplicate is sent to the boy's father, who proceeds at once to make preparations, issue invitations, etc. When the first day arrives the bridegroom, with a procession of his male relatives and friends, proceeds to the bride's house. They are generally accompanied by several musicians, so called, and one or two dancing girls. They also take fireworks, which are let off when they arrive at the bride's house.

The bridegroom then sends his barber on before with a small present. The barber is entertained with sweetmeats, and sent back again. The father of the bride, with some near relatives, then goes out to meet the procession, and when they meet the father touches the feet of the bridegroom, puts a yellow mark on his forehead, and makes him presents. He then washes the bridegroom's feet, and gives him and those who are with him "sherbet," that is, lemonade, to drink.

When the auspicious moment arrives the bridegroom and his friends are received by the bride's father, the bride, and her near relatives in a rude shed that has five props. One of these props is in the center and is very important. After several very trifling rites the priest burns incense, and the bride's father presents the young couple with a piece of yellow cloth each. After several other ceremonies the upper garments of the bride and bridegroom are joined with a knot. Then follows "pooja" and making of presents. The priest then builds a small altar between the central post of the shed and the young couple, and after repeating the names of the sun, fire, water, etc., he burns incense upon it. A near relative of the bridegroom now throws a large cloth over the bride and bridegroom, and quite a round of puerile observances is gone through with. After this the priest of the bride's family addresses the bridegroom as follows:

"The bride says to you, 'If you live happy, keep me happy also; if you are in trouble, I will be in trouble too; you must support me, and must not leave me when I suffer; you must always keep me with you, and pardon all my faults, and you must not perform your religious duties without me; you must not defraud me regarding conjugal love; you must have nothing to do with another woman while I live; you must consult me in all that you do, and you must always tell me the truth; Vishnoo, fire, and the Brahmins are witnesses between you and me.' "

To this the bridegroom replies: "I will all my life do just as the bride requires of me. But she must also make me some promises. She must go with me through suffering and trouble, and must always be obedient to me; she must never go to her father's house unless she is asked by him, and when she sees another in better circumstances or better favored than I am she must not despise or slight me."

To this the bride answers: "I will all my life do just as you require of me; Vishnoo, fire, and the Brahmins are witnesses between us."

After this the bridegroom takes water and sprinkles the bride's head, while the priest repeats invocations. They then both bow before the sun in worship.

After a few more trifling ceremonies the "shadee," as it is called, is completed, and the priest puts a mark on the foreheads of the young pair, blesses them, takes his dues and his departure. The bride and bridegroom then return to their separate homes and live as before, with their parents.

The concluding ceremonies are performed in the third, fifth, seventh, or ninth year succeeding the "shadee." These latter ceremonies constitute the "gauna," or puckah marriage. They are only two in number, and are very simple.

The bride and bridegroom are presented each with a small smooth board; the bride sits on the bridegroom's, and he on that belonging to the bride; then women relatives of the bride put little tinkling bells on her toes, and also place a chudder over her. The bride is then taken away in a little covered vehicle, drawn by two bullocks, to the residence of her husband. When she leaves her friends she is expected to cry bitterly, else it will be said of her that she has no affection for them. I have myself listened to the bride's strange made-up cries as she was being driven off to her new home.

Another tedious round of ceremonies is gone through with upon the arrival of the newly wedded pair at their future residence.

NATAL CEREMONIES.

These begin immediately upon the birth of a child. The family priest is called for at once, who foretells the future of the child without seeing either it or the mother.

After this "Ganesh" and the planets are worshiped, and the father of the child makes presents to the priest and to his relatives. On the sixth day a certain god is believed to come and write the child's future or fate ("kissmat") on its forehead, and they consequently have several ceremonies and a feast for the friends of the family.

At night the women of the family make an image of clay, fasten it against the wall, and worship it. They then put one or two garments on the child, (it has heretofore been merely wrapped in a cloth,) and some rings on its wrists and ancles.

On the twenty-seventh day after the birth of the child they take water from twenty-seven different wells, and twenty-seven different kinds of leaves, and place in an earthen vessel in twenty-seven different compartments. After this, incense is burned, and a blanket is held up over the mother and child and the water from the earthern vessel is poured on the blanket, when it runs through, of course, on to them.

FUNERAL CEREMONIES.

When a person dies his friends present a black cow, or its equivalent in money, to a certain Brahmin whose duty it is to attend to the corpse. Sometimes when a person is dying the leaves of the sacred toolshee tree and some Ganges water are put in his mouth, and a small image of a god called Saligran, on his breast. The dying man then repeats "Ram, Ram."

The Hindoos of Northern India burn their dead. On the death of a man his son, or whoever is to set fire to the funeral pile, makes a ball of some dough of barley-flour and puts it into the right hand of the corpse. The body is wrapped in cloth, placed on a bamboo frame-work, and four men carry it to the place for burning, which is usually by a stream. As they go along they keep repeating "Ram sach hai," "Ram sach hai;" that is, "Ram is true."

When they place the body on the funeral pile they put a little gold and clarified butter into its mouth, and then lay a piece of chandan wood on its breast. The person that sets fire to the pile shaves his face and head, except the tuft of hair on the top, and for ten days must not touch any one.

When the body is half consumed they pour a little ghee on the head and break it with bamboos, and when the flesh is quite consumed, they quench the fire and throw the bones into the Ganges, or if they are at a distance from that stream, they gather the bones and keep them till some member of the family goes to bathe in the "sacred river," when he carries them and casts them into its waters. They clear off the spot where the burning took place, and write Ram, Ram in the sand.

I have made this sketch brief as possible, but I hope not too much so to be uninteresting to you. Please bear in mind that Hindoo ceremonies vary among different castes and localities, and you may meet with descriptions of them differing from these, which are still just as correct. We have never witnessed all the marriage or funeral ceremonies, but wedding processions and burning of corpses are matters of daily occurrence.

SEASONS AND CROPS.

We have, in reality, only three seasons in India, the hot, rainy, and cold; but the terms spring and autumn are often used.

The hot season extends from about the middle of March till the latter part of June, when the rainy season commences and the hot wind subsides. The grains which were sown in October and November are harvested in March and April, and this constitutes the "rubbee," or spring harvest. Wheat, potatoes, peas, etc., ripen at this time.

The trees renew their leaves during these months, but the change is so gradual that it would scarcely be noticed but for the large quantities of dead leaves that are gathered up daily in the groves and used for fuel.

During the hot season dust storms are of frequent occurrence, and are sometimes of great violence. Large trees are split, and even torn up by the roots, and carried some distance. Some years the rains are withheld, and the merchants raise the price of grain till there is much distress among the people. A fine shower will often lower prices considerably. Other years the rains are so plentiful that rivers, tanks, and ponds overflow large tracts of country, and render traveling difficult, and even dangerous. Villages are sometimes swept away, and great destruction of life and property ensues. Reptiles and insects abound, and many die from their bites and stings.

In August and September is the "khareef," or autumn harvest, when Indian cereals, rice, etc., are gathered in. The rains sensibly lessen during these months, and close about the last of September. The sun shines almost continuously, and with great heat, and from the steaming vegetation there rises a malaria that causes much sickness among the people, Europeans as well as natives.

The intervening months between the rainy and hot seasons constitute our cold season, which is delightfully cool and invigorating. Cool bracing nights, and bright sunny days, render existence a luxury and renovate the physical system.

LETTER XIV.

Missionary Work in Budaon — Girls' School — Itineratings — Hot Season — Tattees — Small Pox — Journey to Nynee Tal — Sickness in the Mission — Death of Jesse R. Pierce — Return to Budaon.

BUDAON, April 20, 1860.

MY DEAR MOTHER,—I must tell you in this letter something of our work in this place. Our native catechist is Joseph Angelo, a member of the little society of native Christians belonging to the Church of England at Bareilly. He was formerly a Roman Catholic, but concluded that was but little better than to be a Hindoo, so he became a Protestant. He is a very efficient helper in many respects, but does not possess so much influence among the natives as is desirable. Mary, his wife, is an energetic, capable woman, and a very good teacher.

I commenced a school soon after we came here, on what is called by some the "bribing system," as an experiment. It is extremely difficult to persuade the natives to let their daughters come to us to be taught. They think it wholly unnecessary for women to be able to read, and even regard it as a disreputable acquisition, since dancing girls and others of ques-

Mission Premises at Budaon.

tionable character, are the only ones among them who are possessed of this knowledge.

We try to convince them that their daughters will make better wives and mothers if they are more intelligent; but they answer, "It is all very well for the sahib logue," that is, the white people; "it is your custom, but it is not ours, and we don't wish to change." They object, too, that their girls earn one or two anas a day by picking cotton or gathering sticks, or whatever it may be, and they cannot afford to have them lose two hours every morning for school. So I said to them, "I will pay your girls one pice each for coming to school two hours regularly every day."

I engaged twelve young girls in that way, and could have engaged fifty more, I dare say, but that number was sufficient for the experiment and for the means in hand.

There are also six Christian children, two from one of the Christian families we found here, and four belonging to our native catechist; so I have a school of eighteen children, all girls except three.

We, that is Mary and I, go into the school-room every morning at seven o'clock. We first read and explain a few verses from the Bible, then all join in singing a verse or two and kneel in prayer. After the leading prayer all join in repeating, "Our Father, who art in heaven," etc.

We then teach the children hymns, and the simplest questions of the catechism. These opening exercises occupy about half an hour.

For one hour we then teach them to read and spell, and two or three of the Christian children to write; then half an hour is spent in plain sewing, which they very soon learn. I pay them every Saturday morning six pice each, which make one and a half anas, or four cents and a half!

This sum, though small, is of considerable importance to them, and will help them a great deal, as the cloth and grain they buy are of cheap, coarse quality.

Several of them have paid so much attention to my remarks about cleanliness and neatness in dress, that instead of spending their money for sweetmeats they save up their anas until they have enough to purchase themselves some new article of dress. One appeared in a spotless new chudder, another in a new skirt, etc.

The Christian children learn rapidly, but the twelve little Hindoo children were wild as hares when they began to attend school, and I have found it very difficult to interest them in books. Two or three of them are very bright, and will soon become good scholars; but the others are rather dull.

One morning several of the girls came very late, and when they entered the school-room looked very serious. When I asked what had delayed them, they all came right to me leading one of their number along rather forcibly. They said, "Mem sahib, this girl got very angry and behaved very wickedly; she tried to throw herself in a well!" One of them ventured to say that she would have gone to a very bad place indeed if she had succeeded, didn't the mem sahib think so? I talked with them some time, until the little culprit said she should never, never try to do so wicked a thing again.

Mr. H. and Joseph have a boys' school in the city, with over sixty boys in attendance; but we lack in efficient teachers. Joseph does very well for young boys, but is scarcely advanced enough himself to teach those who, having already learned to read, are ready to take up mathematics, geography, etc.

We have commenced a mission chapel near our house, quite a large sum having been subscribed by the English residents of Budaon for this purpose. This, of course, involves more labor for Mr. H.; but we must have such buildings at our mission stations, and much work of this kind falls necessarily on the pioneer missionary.

The interest manifested in the preaching by the people in the city still continues. They gather by hundreds whenever Mr. H. and Joseph take their stand and commence reading or talking. Often two, three, or four men come up to the Sabbath services on the mission premises. But they all seem very wary, and do not intend to become Christians, nor to be made such by any arts of legerdemain.

The hot wind commenced earlier than usual this year, and we expect a most trying season in consequence. It fairly shrieks around the house, and if by any mischance I catch a stray breath as the servants come in, it seems to scorch my face and eyeballs like the heat of an oven. Night and day the punkahs are kept in motion, and we have also put up what is called a tattee. It is a mat of the fragrant kuskus grass, made on a frame and fitted in a westerly doorway, the door itself being fastened back.

The bheestee keeps this wet by throwing water on it from the outside, and the hot wind rushes through it, transformed into a cool refreshing breeze. The punkah then sends this cooled air all over the house.

This plan would seem to be very desirable, but in our case we found it to be most pernicious. We had colds, catarrhs, and neuralgias in abundance, and were obliged to give it up.

Small-pox broke out in Budaon the first of this month, and spread rapidly among the swarming multitudes in the city. An English gentleman in the house next to us had it quite severely, and it also made its appearance on our own premises in the family of the sweeper. He continued, however, to come to his work daily, until we learned of the state of affairs from our catechist, and forbade him the house.

Europeans are not so fearful of this dread disease as our people at home, or else, like the Orientals, they have learned to submit patiently to their "kismat." No one seems to think of taking any further precaution than to see that every member of the family is vaccinated.

Native vaccinators are also sent forth from the hospitals into the cities and villages to vaccinate the people, and thousands submit to the operation, although they are somewhat afraid of it. Some are suspicious that in some mysterious way the Christian religion may be infused! Others suspect it is to test people's loyalty, and suppose that the vaccinators can tell from the quality of the blood who are friends to government and who are foes! We hear of some sickness in our mission even so early in the season.

When we removed to this place Mr. and Mrs. Waugh removed from Shahjehanpore to Bareilly, and Mr. Baume and family removed from Lucknow to Shahjehanpore. A daughter was born to them in February, and has recently died. They are alone in the mission at S., as are we here. So long as we remain well we do not mind being alone so very much, as constant occupation keeps us from loneliness; but there is always a trembling anxiety when illness comes, and a strong desire for the presence of other missionaries.

Mrs. Parker, of Bijnour, has been suffering from severe illness, and has already been obliged to take refuge in Nynee Tal. My own health begins to suffer from the intense heat, and we have concluded that I ought to spend May and June in the hills, and so escape the debilitating effect of the hot wind.

NYNEE TAL, June 11, 1860.

You perceive, dear mother, there is quite a gap in my dates. My health failed so rapidly that I left Budaon sooner than I expected. Mr. H. took me over to Bareilly in his buggy, and after a delightful visit with our friends, sent me alone from there to Nynee Tal.

I left Bareilly at nine o'clock P. M., and had a lonely journey in my palkee to Rampore, which I reached in about twelve hours. I stopped at the little dak bungalow which the nawab of Rampore keeps open for the accommodation of European travelers. The heat was so intense I could only remain quietly in the bungalow all day, till the evening coolness should enable me to go on.

The servants were very respectful and attentive, but I could not help feeling ill at ease through the day.

The khansamah brought me an excellent dinner, and a cup of tea just as I was about to leave, but would accept no payment, it was against "his highness's" orders; and, wonder of wonders! the ever-ready cry of "buksheesh" was also missing. The servants, however, did not refuse a small present each, and made me profound salams when I departed.

I traveled the ensuing night without further incident than the requests for buksheesh whenever the kahars changed, and the screams of jackals. I reached Kaludoongee, at the foot of the hills, about eight o'clock in the morning, where I found nine paharees and a jhaumpaun waiting for me. Half way up the hill I found our bachelor missionary, Mr. Thoburn, who had kindly come down to meet me.

I was glad to see the cheerful green little valley and grand old hills of Nynee Tal again, and O how invigorating were the deliciously cool mountain breezes! The lake looked greener and smaller than ever, and the cottages on the mountain slopes were resplendent with new paint. The lieutenant-governor and his suite are spending the season here, and the buildings have been put in better repair than usual, perhaps on that account.

Mr. Knowles and family occupy half the mission house, and the other half has had quite a number of occupants since I came up. Mr. and Mrs. Parker, Dr. Butler and family, Mrs. Pierce and children, Mr. Humphrey and myself, have helped to keep the rooms well filled. Dr. Butler's family remained only a week, with the exception of their two boys, who are still in my care.

Mrs. Pierce came the sixteenth of May, in the vain hope of saving the life of her little boy of eighteen months. He had been very healthy until he came to the ordeal of teething, and even then kept pretty well until the hot weather came on, when he was seized with fever. The sweet little sufferer was too far gone to rally. He lived only nine days after they arrived. You can understand somewhat how sad it was for Mrs. Pierce to bury her darling here alone. She suffered much in her own health from her unremitting care of the child, and after he was buried she was ill for several days. She was able to acquiesce sweetly in the divine will, although her heart was sorely stricken by the bereavement. She and little Rilla have returned to Lucknow. Mr. and Mrs. Parker have also returned to Bijnour.

Mr. Humphrey came up the last of May. We intend to return to Budaon so soon as the "chota barsat" shall have quenched the scorching raging winds that are sweeping over the plains.

I am advised to remain here through the season, but I do not like to be separated from my husband longer than is absolutely necessary, and my health is so much improved now that I hope to remain well throughout the season.

LETTER XV.

Unusual Heat — Drought — Famine — Strange Vagaries of Hindooism — Service of the Church of England — Anglo-Vernacular School — School for Boys of the Sweeper Caste — Illness — A Friend in Need — Convalescence — Hindòo Fair — Cold Season — Famine Orphans — Christmas Observances — Annual Meeting — Removal to Bareilly.

BUDAON, August 15, 1860.

MY DEAR MOTHER,—Immediately after the first rain fell in June we left Nynee Tal for Budaon, where we arrived on the morning of the 27th. Instead of the usual rains through July and August, we have only had occasional showers, which cool the atmosphere temporarily, but have little effect upon the earth.

There is, therefore, much distress among the people, as the grain merchants promptly brought the prices up to famine rates. Many poor people have sold their children to rich men, for two and three rupees each, openly in our streets! There have also been cases of robbery and committal to jail, when the only motive of the offender was to get into a place where he would receive food?

Our mischievous neighbors, the apes, make frequent forays into the blighted crops to appease their hunger, although, wonderful as it may seem, the grain merchants bring bags of wheat to the groves inhabited by these creatures, and feed them, while men, women, and children are starving all around. They are under no obligation to feed people of low caste, but apes must not be allowed to suffer! They also place grain, sugar, and salt by the ant hills for the benefit of ants!

I have not been able to recommence my school since my return, as my health is so unreliable at this season.

Mr. H. holds the boys' Anglo-vernacular school in our chapel now, which is finished and dedicated. It is a small "puckah" building with a portico in front. We hold Hindoostanee services in it every Sabbath morning, and English services in the evening. I have not mentioned to you, I think, that we have held a service in English ever since we have been here. The occasion of it is this: there is no chaplain stationed here, and the few European residents wished Mr. H. to hold one service on the Sabbath for them. He reads the service of the Church of England and delivers a short discourse.

We have a boys' school in the city, pupiled wholly by boys of the mihtar, or sweeper caste, the lowest strata of Hindooism. The poor lads have had much difficulty in getting into mixed schools on account of their degraded condition, so they have come into this school in numbers so large as to monopolize it.

Joseph Angelo has returned to Bareilly, and we have in his stead Enoch Burge, a native preacher, formerly of the American Presbyterian Mission in Futteghur. He has an excellent wife, three intelligent sons, and one little daughter.

BARIELLY, May 21, 1861.

MY DEAR MOTHER,—I am grateful to my heavenly Father that I am permitted to write you again. He has raised me from the bed of sickness, and restored me to a good degree of health again. I suffered from fever most of the early part of September, 1860, and was in consequence prematurely confined of a son on the 13th. He remained with us only a few days, and then the little pure spirit returned to Him who gave it.

This deep disappointment and sorrow, added to the depressing influence of the intense heat, was of course unfavorable to me, and to my husband's grief at our loss was soon added great anxiety on my account.

The day our little one was buried I began to suffer excessively from faintness and difficulty of breathing, and at one time I was so very low that I gave up all hope of recovery. For several days I hovered on the borders of the spirit-world; but it pleased God to so bless the remedies used, and the tender care I was favored with, that I began to rally, and after a tedious convalescence recovered my strength.

Our dear, kind friend, Mrs. Waugh, came over from Bareilly immediately upon hearing of my illness, and remained until I began decidedly to mend. You may well believe she was a great comfort to us both through this trying season.

Clara, Enoch's wife, was also very kind, and manifested so much love and sympathy that I felt my heart not only drawn out more strongly toward her, but also toward native women generally, since I had such proof of their true womanliness and capacity for good.

Toward the last of November the usual melas, or fairs, were held by the Hindoos at different points on the Ganges.

Mr. Knowles, who removed to Bareilly in October last, and Joseph Fieldbrave, came over and accompanied Mr. H. and Enoch Burge to that point on the Ganges where the people assembled from this region of country. They had a stirring time at the great mela, preaching to multitudes and distributing tracts and gospels. It was estimated that at least one hundred and fifty thousand people were present.

The cold season was delightful, and but for the continued famine our surroundings would have been so; but it was very painful to witness so much suffering that we could do but little to alleviate. The English residents have raised a relief fund, from which distributions of rice, flour, etc, are made daily; but as these distributions are in the cities, the poor villagers in the district cannot profit much by it, and many have died from starvation. We are beginning to gather famine orphans into our orphanages. Two boys have been recently forwarded to Bareilly by us. Their case is quite interesting. They came to our verandah one cold bright morning in December, and startled me, as I was reading quietly by the fire, by a sharp plaintive call, "Mem sahib, we are dying from hunger! please give us food." I went out and found two boys, evidently not professional beggars, shivering in the keen air. The elder boy looked about ten years of age, and had a frank, earnest countenance. A bundle of tattered garments was tied to his neck, in order that his arms might be free to carry the other boy, a poor emaciated child apparently about two years of age. The hungry look in their eyes went to my heart.

"Will you eat some bread?" I asked, for I saw they were Hindoos, but I could not tell their caste.

"O yes!" said the elder boy, "I will be very glad to, and so will my brother, for he can't eat the coarse bread which the people sometimes give us."

I gave them each a slice of bread, and told them to sit down and eat, and afterward they could tell me why they came to the mission house. They had said they were from a village ten miles away.

"We want to stay here," spoke up the elder boy at once.

The little boy scarcely knew whether the strange, light white substance was designed to be eaten or not. He ate a small piece, and finding it to be very good, stuffed his mouth so full that he could not chew it. So his brother kindly broke off small mouthfuls, and fed him the whole piece before he ate his own.

Their story was a sad one. "A long time ago," said the elder boy, "I don't know how long, my father and mother died of starvation. They had been weak and ill for some time, and then there was no one to go begging for food but me, and I did not get much, for the neighbors were all so poor. One morning, when my little brother and I awoke, they were both dead. I carried my brother to a neighbor's house, and used to take him all around to the villagers and beg for food. The people were very kind, and always shared their food with us, and, till the grass dried up so that the cows gave no milk, they gave my brother milk occasionally. When we could no longer get a little milk, I sometimes got rice or a little dal, and boiled till very tender, and fed him, but now for many days I could get only coarse bread, and so he has become very thin and ill. Two days ago a man told me that there was a padre sahib in Budaon who took orphan children and provided for them, so I have brought my brother all the way in my arms, and we may stay here, mayn't we?" I assured him that he might, if his story proved to be true, and I sent a servant with them at once to make inquiries at the police station. He ascertained that they were really orphans, and wholly destitute of friends, so there was nothing to prevent our taking charge of them. We kept them over a week in order to make up some clothes for them, and to give the little one time to recruit. It was touching to see the rare unselfishness of Gulab, the elder boy. He seemed grateful for his own good food and clothing, but appeared to take far more delight in his brother's bettered circumstances. "In a few days," said he, "he will be able to walk again, and then he will grow fat and strong. When they left for Bareilly he could walk a little, and the starved expression was gone from his eyes; but he will probably never be very strong.

Christmas morning gifts came pouring in from our Hindoostanee teachers and friends in the city, and we learned that the natives, knowing this to be a "burra din," that is, a great day with Europeans, usually make them presents and pay them their respects on that day. The gifts are generally flat baskets tastefully covered with lemons, oranges, pomegranates, raisins, almonds, grapes, and small cones of white sugar. A servant bearing the presents usually precedes the donor, who, having deposited the basket on the floor near the "sahib," quietly retires. The native gentleman then comes to the door, where he takes off his shoes and enters the room barefoot. He does not uncover his head, however, as that would be considered a mark of disrespect. He then bows nearly to the floor, at the same time raising his right hand to his forehead, and says, "Salam, sahib," that is, Peace be with you, sir. After he is seated he inquires, "Is your honor's temper good?" after which they chat on various subjects. It is not allowable to ask after a person's health unless he is ill, and on no account may you ask a native gentleman if his wife and children are well. If on very intimate terms with him you may inquire if his house are well, meaning of course its inmates. Indeed, there is no word in the Hindoostanee language to express the relation of wife.

Just here let me explain. As a general rule a native does not make a present from mere good-will. He has usually some good to himself in view. Give, "hoping for nothing again," is no part of his creed. It would rather run, "Give, hoping to receive threefold."

Our teachers would like higher salaries, our servants higher wages, or, what they value more, "buksheesh." Our native acquaintances see that we are on friendly term with the magistrates and judges, and so think it politic to propitiate us, as they may some time wish to have the benefit of our influence with those magnates. There are, however, exceptions to this rule. Many natives undoubtedly are sincerely attached to the missionaries, and believe them to be promoting the welfare of the people.

We held service about midday, and in the evening all met in the chapel again and had a little entertainment, designed more particularly for the six children of our little community, but which the adults seemed to enjoy as well.

The doors of the chapel were festooned with wreaths of green leaves, and some presents for the children were hung on a small tree which had been purloined from a grove hard by. Oranges, lemons, and confectionary helped to give the tree a very captivating appearance to the eyes of the children.

We all partook of cakes and tea first, after which Enoch went into the altar, and, with many witty remarks about the singular tree which bore so many kinds of fruit, distributed the gifts. As there were several presents for each of the children, they had quite a merry time going to the altar to receive them, and then making their salams in acknowledgement.

When the distribution was over, Enoch's two eldest boys repeated some hymns and portions of Scripture, and we all joined in singing a Christmas hymn to the tune of "Happy Day," which, with a deal of trouble in the selection of words, I had composed for the occasion.

After prayer we separated, well pleased with the result of the little effort put forth to commemorate the day.

January passed away without note, except that Mr. Cowie, the chaplain of Bareilly, came over to Budaon and held communion service for the English residents. It was a very pleasant season. We were allowed to join with members of *the* Church this time, in commemorating the death and sufferings of our common Lord. Mr. Cowie handed over the sacramental collection to Mr. Humphrey for the mission school.

We visited a famous temple one day, the only one of note in the city, which is now used as a mosque by Mohammedans. It is said to be a very ancient edifice, built by the Hindoos, but wrested from them by the Mohammedans. Outwardly it is merely a plain large temple, brown and mossy with age, but the interior is beautiful.

Under the immense dome is a large room enclosed only on three sides, the fourth opening on a spacious platform, which, with the floor of the room, is paved with marble. The walls are covered with quaint and beautiful mouldings and frescoes, and in numerous places are inscribed with the name of God—Allah.

The Mohammedans shame us by their open attachment to their religion. No matter what a faithful Mussulman is doing, when the muezzin's cry sounds out from the mosques he drops his work or ceases to bargain, and turning his face toward Mecca, bows humbly to the ground and repeats a formula of prayer.

Many things indeed meet our eyes daily that remind us that the Bible is an Eastern book. This Mohammedan custom of praying in the streets and shops is very like that of the proud Pharisees, who prayed to be seen of men.

All the grains are ground by hand-mills, and the work is mostly done by women, the aged mothers and widows. We hear the "sound of the grinding" early in the morning as we pass the houses of the natives, and we are reminded of the passage, "Two women shall be grinding at the mill, the one shall be taken and the other left."

Then, too, the women of the lower castes come to the wells to draw water, bearing their curiously-shaped pitchers (ghurrahs) on their heads, like Rebekah of old. The flat roofs of the "puckah" houses—whither the natives, especially the women, resort in the evening—the bridal processions, all seem strangely natural to us, so like are they to the scenes delineated in holy writ.

The first of February we started for Bareilly, where our annual meeting was to be held. We traveled by marches, making but ten miles a day, Mr. H. and Enoch preaching by the way. We reached Bareilly the third day, and pitched our tent on the new mission premises near cantonments which are now adorned by a very fine kotee occupied by Dr. Butler. Another house, a bungalow, was in process of erection, and also some buildings for the boys' orphanage.

On the mission "compound," as such inclosures are called here, several tents were standing, for we were each to "keep house," and meet in Dr. Butler's library for our sessions and religious services. Our missionary band were all present except Mrs. Judd and Mr. Thoburn. Mr. Parsons had gone out from us. He left early in the year and joined a Baptist mission.

The annual meeting was very interesting. Joel, Enoch, Thomas, Zahoor-ul-Huqq, and two or three other native catechists preached, and several orphan boys were baptized. Mrs. Pierce and Mrs. Downey gave very favorable accounts of the state of the orphanages. The missionaries reported their fields of labor, schools, converts, inquirers, etc.

When we broke up it was with a feeling of deep sympathy for each other and of united interest in our work.

As we were appointed to Bareilly, I did not return to Budaon. I spent most of the interim between the annual meeting and Mr. Humphrey's return with our goods, at Cashmere Kotee. When he arrived we pitched a large tent and occupied it till the first of March, when Dr. Butler removed his family to Nynee Tal, and we took possession of part of the house they had occupied.

The first week of April Mr. and Mrs. Waugh and Mrs. Downey, with the orphan boys and the whole staff of native teachers and servants, moved over from Cashmere Kotee.

Mrs. Downey caught a severe cold while moving, which speedily brought her down with inflammation of the lungs. For two weeks she lay very ill, and then was just able to be placed in a palkee and taken to Nynee Tal. We feared when she left that she might not live to reach there.

Mrs. Waugh accompanied her, and remained by her a fortnight. She then returned home, leaving Mrs. Downey, who was slowly recovering, to spend the season.

Mr. H. and I each had an attack of fever in April. He recovered very quickly, but I remained so weak, and had symptoms so alarming, that our physician hurried me off to Nynee Tal. I recovered very rapidly there, and returned home after a stay of three weeks.

I found still another bungalow in process of erection on my return, and was informed that it was to be our house.

The season is now in the very zenith of its heat, but we do not find it so very difficult to keep comfortable as we did last year. We study a great deal, and Mr. H. is kept very busy in superintending the workmen on the orphanage and printing office and the new bungalow, and in preaching in the city.

This place seems strangely home-like, I presume because here we first launched out into the native work. If another Zahoor-ul-Huqq be granted us this year we shall rejoice.

LETTER XVI.

Startling News from Home — Girls' School — Arrangement of Native Work in Bareilly — Effect of Preaching — Inquirer — His Persecutions — Conversion — Narrowly escapes Martyrdom — Liberality of English Residents — Building — Heavy Rains — Wesleypore Colony — Removal to Shahjehanpore.

SHAHJEHANPORE, Nov. 21, 1861.

MY DEAR MOTHER,—Before I resume my account of our life in Bareilly I must notice the startling news from home.

We received news of the outrage at Fort Sumter by telegraph about the middle of May, and the last papers we received in June brought the terrible news that war with the South is inevitable. How strange it seems! Our own peaceful land at war, brother with brother! It seemed to us when we first read the news, that the foundations of the earth were being moved! It appears to us here that this struggle involves more than it purports to at present; in fact, that it will not cease until that deadly blight upon our fair land, that shameful stigma upon our republican institutions, slavery, is removed.

The Christian world has been looking for this eruption. It could not but come, since God hears the cry of the oppressed and will avenge them.

You may well believe that we are, and shall be, very anxious. The mails will be impatiently waited for, but when received will be, alas! two months old. But I will go on with my narrative.

Soon after I returned from Nynee Tal I commenced a girls' school, in which were some twelve pupils, including the native preacher's and servant's girls and three or four young Sikh women. I commenced the school the first of June, and kept it up till October. I did not pay any one for attending, but during one hour each day I had them sew on garments for the orphan boys, and paid them according to their work.

The girls improved fast in sewing, with this incentive before them, and several of them earned eight or ten annas per week. An anna equals three cents. Minepul Sing's young wife excelled the others. She was an ignorant young girl when Minepul brought her to the Mission the previous winter, and he was very anxious to have her learn to read and sew, and more than all he strongly desired her to understand and believe the Christian religion. She was very awkward at first, and I often despaired of her learning the alphabet of her own language; and as to sewing, her needle went in every direction except the right one. I don't really know whether she or I had the harder time of it during the first month of the school, but she came up all right at last, and earned three annas a day, by sewing, a good part of the season. Her mind expanded proportionately. She learned to read, and seemed in some measure to comprehend and feel the force of the truths of Christianity.

The first hour of school was always deeply interesting. The women and elder girls sat on low cane seats on one side, and the younger girls on a rug on the other, forming a three-quarter's circle around me.

The lesson was always something about the life of our Saviour, but often, through their numerous and curious questions, extended back to the deluge and forward to the resurrection day! After this we all joined in singing a simple hymn, and in learning two or three others. Then we all knelt in prayer, and in conclusion all joined in repeating our Lord's prayer.

My school hours, from six o'clock till nine A. M., were the happiest of the day. I became greatly attached to my scholars, and had the satisfaction of seeing them improve very much. One little girl, named Gunguah, is the daughter of our sais, and was so destitute of suitable clothing that, in order to have her fit to attend the school, I gave her a school dress, and required her to wear it only during school hours. Her parents are Hindoos, and do not like to have her learn to read, as they fear she will become tainted with the "new religion."

Another bright little girl, daughter of a native

preacher, had always been very wild and averse to school. She commenced coming, but her mother told me she presumed I would find it quite impossible to interest her, and that probably she would only attend a few days. But no! she applied herself diligently, learned to read and sew, and became so attached to the school that she would linger about the hall door an hour before the time for opening.

I did little else through the season but attend to my school, as my health remained unsettled. Still, I was conscious of making rapid advancement in the language. I usually listened while Mr. H. read with the moonshee, and thus received some of the benefit of the lesson without the labor. He was so well known in Bareilly, too, that he received many native visitors, and I found great pleasure in listening to their conversations. I was often surprised at the clearness with which the intricate distinctions laid down in the grammars were brought out in them.

I gave as much attention as possible to the translation of hymns, but found it exceedingly difficult to accomplish anything satisfactorily. However, I succeeded in changing the dress of sixteen of our standard hymns during the year.

The native work, as a whole, was more interesting this year than we had ever known it before. We had a very efficient staff of native helpers, who, although engaged in different departments of the work, were able to alternate in bazar preaching and visiting among the natives.

Enoch Burge was the native preacher. Caleb, whom we knew in Calcutta, and who is an excellent preacher, had come to us as an assistant to Mr. Waugh in the work of the mission printing press. Thomas Cullen was engaged in the boys' orphanage.

Every Monday morning these native preachers met with the missionaries, and a plan for the week's preaching was made out and a copy given to each. Every evening in the week there was preaching at some point in or about the city. A system of visiting native gentlemen at their houses was also begun, and adhered to during our stay in Bareilly.

Mr. Cowie also placed the little society of native Christians under his care in our charge, with a view to their being permanently included in our mission. Joseph Angelo alternated with our preachers in the city work, and some one of our staff held service in their little village every Sabbath morning. There was also a band of Eurasians, attached to a native regiment stationed in Bareilly, with whom we held service once a week.

This constant stirring up of the native mind necessarily produced some effect. The preaching in the bazars was very largely attended, and many discussions were held. The large number of college students, some of whom were very regular attendants upon the preaching, rendered the congregations unusually intelligent. There were many who seemed convinced of the truth of Christianity, but yet could not make up their minds to break away from their friends, and the ties of caste and superstition.

One young baboo, (Hindoo gentleman,) however, was led to "count all things but loss," that he might "win Christ." He had listened to the preaching several times the first year we were in Bareilly, and when we returned he began to call on Mr. H. and converse with him freely about the way of salvation. He then commenced attending the Hindoostanee services, although, in order to elude the vigilance of his father-in-law, who was bitterly opposed to Christianity, he was sometimes obliged to come in undress. He was not watched so closely before dressing, as his father-in-law supposed he would not think of visiting the "Padre sahib" without being properly clothed. I have seen him tremble with emotion during the sermon, and it was evident that the spirit of God was striving with him, and what a struggle it must have been! How little do those in our own land who talk about giving up the world and sacrificing their pleasures, etc., know about real self-denial! Umbeeka Churn, the young baboo, finally resolved he would be a Christian at all hazards. His praying and reading of the Bible soon raised his father-in-law's wrath to such a pitch that he could not endure it. Several times he was severely beaten, and he resolved that as he could not serve the Lord in peace at home he would flee to the mission. He reasoned with his young wife, and prevailed upon her to accompany him. One morning they fled, but were discovered and followed. The timid young wife was forced to return by her father, but the baboo came to the mission. The same night a part of his friends came and demanded him, but he was not forthcoming. Early the next morning the father-in-law came to our house and desired Mr. H. to allow the baboo to come on to the verandah and converse with him. As he was alone, and seemed very calm and dispassionate, Mr. H. sent for the baboo and two native Christians. They came, sat down in the verandah, and began to converse quite amicably. After a few minutes Mr. H. came into the house for the customary cup of tea.

We were scarcely seated at table when a loud blow and a fall resounded from the verandah. We ran out and saw the young man just rising from the floor. Blood was streaming over his face from a wound just over one of his eyes. His father-in-law was running away from the premises. He had first urged the baboo to return home, and upon his refusing, suddenly shrieked out with ungovernable fury, "I am ready to be hung for you," and attempted to strike him on on the temple with a heavy cane. Fortunately the baboo turned his head, and so received the blow on his forehead.

Toward night a rajah from the city, a Hindoo of considerable wealth and influence, and quite a friend of Europeans, came to us, being sent by the baboo's friends, to persuade him to spend the night at the rajah's house in order to hold a discussion with the best pundits the city affords. Mr. H. is acquainted with the rajah and knows him to be at least outwardly honorable. He gave his word that no violence should be used, and that the young man should be returned to the Mission the next morning safe and sound. "I will not deceive you," said the rajah; "we shall do our best to convince the young man that it will be better for him to remain a Hindoo, and we shall probably succeed." He knew well the avarice of the native character, and thought to buy the youth easily; but he did not understand how valueless money looks to a Christian when hung in the balance against his soul.

Mr. H. called the baboo, explained the rajah's design to him, and asked him what he would do. "Sahib," said he, "I do not wish to go; it will be very trying, though I am not afraid that anything they can say will influence me in the least. I will do as you think best."

He went, and that night we all prayed earnestly that God would strengthen him in his hour of trial. We slept but little that night, and next morning all watched anxiously for the rajah to keep his promise. At last his fine horses and carriage were seen approaching bringing the baboo, accompanied by the rajah's son.

We received the baboo back joyfully. He seemed weary, but there was no mistaking the look of satisfaction and peace on his face.

"Are you going to be a Christian, baboo?" asked Mr. H.

"I am," he replied, "the grace of God helping me."

"So, then, you failed to convince the baboo that it would be better for him to remain a Hindoo," said Mr. H. to the rajah's son, who remained in the carriage.

"It is very wonderful," he replied, throwing up his hands with a gesture of astonishment; "who can tell what has got hold of him that he thus throws himself away!" and with a hasty salam he drove off.

All that night had the baboo been assailed by entreaty, argument, and temptation. A desirable situation with a large salary, and with permission to be a Christian privately, was offered him, but he never once wavered, and the rajah himself admitted that he must be sincere in his belief.

The baboo tried every available means to obtain his wife, but in vain. When she was forced to appear in court and declare before the magistrate whether she would go with her husband or not, she said she would not live with him if he would be a Christian. She was probably overawed by her father's threats.

The fact that a baboo had actually broken through the bonds of caste, and, in spite of the determined opposition of his friends, identified himself with the mission, and received Christian baptism, speedily became known throughout the city, and created great excitement.

The people, however, were more attentive to the preaching than ever, and many inquiries were made of the missionaries and native preachers.

There seemed indeed to be an unusual influence moving upon the native mind. The native preachers remarked it, and were led themselves to a greater degree of earnestness and zeal in their efforts to enlighten the people and lead them to the Saviour. There was a depth and fervor in our services on the mission premises that reminded us of seasons of revival at home, and we could but believe that the Spirit of God was working among the people.

We were abundantly supplied with means to

carry on our schools and work in Bareilly by the liberality of the English residents. Several gave us handsome donations, and others gave a certain sum monthly, especially to carry on the local work in Bareilly.

We observed the fast of August fifth, appointed by President Lincoln. Our national flag was raised, as it is indeed every Sabbath. It was very gratifying to us to witness the interest manifested by our native Christians and preachers in the fearful struggle which is going on in our own beloved land, and to listen to their fervent prayers that the right may prevail and peace be speedily restored.

We received notice in September that we must remove from Bareilly to Shahjehanpore the first of November. We had fully expected to remain much longer in Bareilly, and were very sorry to have our relation to this interesting work so soon broken off. We are strongly attached to Bareilly as it was our first mission-field, and we have labored there longer than in any other place, and formed many acquaintances both among Europeans and natives.

There, too, we have seen Zahoor-ul-Huqq, Umbeeka Churn, and several others, break through the time-honored chains of darkness, and emerge into the light of Gospel liberty, and it seemed to us that many others were about to follow their example.

In October Mr. and Mrs. Parker removed to Luckempore, in Oude, about sixty miles from Shahjehanpore, which is the last mission station in Rohilkund.

About twenty miles from Luckempore a settlement has been formed of some of the Sikh inquirers from Moradabad, which is under Mr. Parker's care. These people have continued to manifest a spirit of inquiry, and many among them have become Christians, some of them very earnest ones.

About one hundred people went to this settlement, which is named Wesleypore. Among them were most of the Sikh families we had employed in Bareilly, including Minepul Sing and his wife. Minepul's twin brother, Goordial, and his wife, were also of the number. The object of this is to have a village where, free from the influence and interference of Hindoos and Mohammedans, the people can be Christianized and civilized. Our only fear is that the site is a bad one. It is too near the belt of jungle or wild land that skirts the Himalayas to be a healthy location.

Soon after we removed to Bareilly our mission was reinforced by the arrival of six missionaries: Mr. and Mrs. Hauser, who went direct to Bijnour; Mr. and Mrs. Jackson, who were appointed to Luckempore; Mr. Messmore and Miss Husk, who were both stationed in Lucknow.

Soon after their arrival Mr. Gracy, with his wife and child, arrived, and was located at Seetapore, midway between Lucknow and Shahjehanpore. Luckempore is but twenty miles from Seetapore in a northerly direction. Mr. Jackson has now removed to Bareilly, and assumed the duties of treasurer to the mission.

We came to Shahjehanpore by palkee dak, and arrived late in the evening. We had heard much of the fine mission house here, and when we saw walls striped with black mould, and torn and musty cloth chuts over the rooms, we began to think there must be a mistake somewhere. An examination into the state of affairs, however, showed us that the trouble was all caused by a leaky roof, so we are again involved in all the trouble of repairing a house while we live in it.

Fortunately this is a double bungalow, and while one part is being repaired we can live in the other; but of course the whole house will be strewn with mortar and whitewash, and be redolent of the odors of new tiles and bricks.

The fatigue of moving, and our uncomfortable situation here, have had an unfavorable influence upon my health. I can keep up only part of the day, but I hope to rally soon in this invigorating weather. The delightful cold season is again here, and day after day we rejoice in cold bracing nights and mild balmy days.

LETTER XVII.

Marriage of Mr. Thoburn to Mrs. Downey — Translating Hymns — Mr. Ulman — Reminiscences of the Mutiny in Shahjehanpore — Luckimpore — Mrs. Pierce — Dr. Kareem Buksh — Baptisms — Persecution of Native Christians — Visit to some Native Women — Journey to Nynee Tal — Illness — Return Home — Death of Mrs. Jackson — Death of Mrs. Thoburn — Journey to Bareilly — Death of Mrs. Pierce.

SHAHJEHANPORE, Oct. 25. 1862.

MY DEAR MOTHER,—On the fourteenth of December, 1861, Mr. Thoburn was married to Mrs. Downey at Mr. Waugh's residence in Bareilly. She has given up her connection with the boys' orphanage, and returned with her husband to Nynee Tal. We hope the hill climate may permanently restore her health, which is far from being re-established.

I gradually grew stronger as the cold season advanced, and although suffering constantly, I was able to give some attention to translating hymns. I first revised the sixteen I had on hand, and sent them to Mr. Ulman, of the American Presbyterian Mission, for criticism. He has been engaged in Hindoostanee hymnology for over twenty years, and is the best authority on the subject in Northern India. He very kindly criticised my hymns freely, pointed out defects, and gave me some very grateful words of commendation and encouragement. Mr. Scott too, of the same mission, was so kind as to read the hymns, and to send me words of encouragement to go on in the work of translating.

Mr. Ulman also gave me some hints in regard to the styles of rhyme peculiar to this language, etc. I have since worked with much greater facility, as I have a more definite idea in regard to what I wish to attain.

Enoch Burge and his family accompanied us to Shahjehanpore. We found here three men who professed to be Christians. One was in the police, and made an open profession of his belief. The other two were endeavoring to be Christians by stealth.

There was a boys' school, with an average attendance of fifteen, in the little chapel Mr. Cawdell built in 1861. A young native Christian from Lucknow was in charge of it. Mr. H. soon removed the school to the city, where he obtained a fine large building in a good situation for it. The number of scholars increased so rapidly that he had no Christian teacher, capable of managing so large a school, who could be spared for that work. He engaged a young baboo, who proved to be an excellent teacher. This young man has a large salary, which, with the rent of the building, etc., makes the expenses of the school quite heavy, and in order to meet them Mr. H. sent a subscription paper to the English residents of the station. They subscribed handsomely, and thus enabled him to bring the school up to a high degree of excellence, and to carry on the work without embarrassment.

Shahjehanpore is a rambling city of about seventy thousand inhabitants, many of whom are Mohammedans. There are no temples or mosques of particular note, although several are of very showy architecture. The outside of one temple is covered with caricatures of fish moulded in plaster and gilded.

The mission house stands very near the city. It is a large commodious bungalow, and stands in an extensive compound, which includes a beautiful garden. There are lemons, oranges, custard apples, pears, peaches, mangoes, and guavas in their season, and a variety of flowers. The roses are finer than any I ever saw before, even at home. There are numbers of the large double roses, several of the scarlet velvet-leaved monthly that we cherish so carefully in-doors at home, and one immense bush which bears a profusion of the loveliest white roses imaginable.

There are also two or three flowering trees that are magnificent. On one, the leaves grow in clusters, in the centers of which are six or eight flesh-colored lily-shaped wax flowers of peculiar fragrance. Another tree has large white

Mission Premises at Shahjehanpore.

flowers similar to the double hollyhock. Clusters of large oleanders stand in rows on two sides of the garden.

We spent Christmas at Luckempore with Mr. and Mrs. Parker and Mr. and Mrs. Pierce. Mrs. Pierce thought the journey might be beneficial to her health, and it was in like hope that I made the tour, as well as to see our friends.

The missionaries all went out to Wesleypore, and were highly pleased with the prosperity of the little Christian community, and much gratified at the indications of improvement which they saw among them.

After a day or two we all went up to Seetapore, and spent several days, in company with Mr. and Mrs. Gracey, at a large fair which was held near Seetapore, at the city of Khairabad.

The missionaries preached daily, and distributed tracts and gospels. It was not a religious but an industrial fair, something after the style of our county fairs at home, and samples of every kind of native growth and manufacture were present in abundance.

There were some famine orphan girls waiting in Seetapore to be taken to Lucknow, and as they were ill Mrs. Pierce was obliged to leave with them before the fair closed. She left in a buggy with 'Rilla and her little son a few months old, and his nurse. The orphans were in doolies. She went in this way to Lucknow, a distance of sixty miles, with but two servants. I felt strangely moved as I saw her leave, she seemed so fragile and spiritual, and so forgetful of self; but I little thought I should not look upon her face again.

Soon after our return home, Mr. H. and Enoch made a tour of thirty miles to visit a Christian zamindar, or landed proprietor. He was also a surgeon, and had formerly been employed in that capacity by the East India Company. In one of the regiments where he served he became acquainted with a pious officer, who instructed him in the principles of the Christian religion and urged him to study the Bible. He told Mr. H. that for years he had been fully convinced of the truth of Christianity, but that he had been deterred from making a public profession of his faith on account of his numerous and bigoted Mohammedan friends, who would not have hesitated to take his life if he had done so. But as the strong arm of the law is now pledged to protect the life and property of such persons, he did not wish to delay any longer. He desired to serve the Lord with all his house.

Dr. Kareem Buksh had himself been baptized some time previously by Mr. Mengee, of the Church Mission in Lucknow. He invited Mr. H. to visit him at this time to baptize his aged mother and a little son who was in delicate health. A crowd of people gathered about the door while the ordinance was being administered. The doctor shed tears of joy while he fervently thanked God that his mother had been enabled to profess her faith in Christ by holy baptism. Afterward Mr. H. and Enoch preached in a large village near by to an attentive multitude. Many among them could read, and were eager to obtain books and tracts. They visited the ancient city of Shahabad, about sixteen miles from Shahjehanpore, on their way home, where they preached to large and deeply interested congregations.

In February our quiet was broken by the welcome arrival of Mr. and Mrs. Thomas from home. They remained six months at Shahjehanpore. Mr. and Mrs. Brown, who came with them, went on to Moradabad. Mr. and Mrs. Hicks, also their fellow-passengers over, were stationed at Luckempore. As the cold season wore away (all too quickly) there seemed to be a general and increasing interest in the preaching among the people. Many incidents occurred from time to time during the bazar preachings that would be amusing, did they not show in so striking a manner how dark and ignorant are the minds around us. I will relate one of them.

One evening, after Mr. H. and Enoch had

been preaching to a large and attentive crowd in the bazar, an aged man came to Mr. H. just as he was about to leave and said, "You have preached God to us good."

Mr. H. replied, "It is necessary that we should obey him."

"Yes," said the old man, "and his prophet also."

"Who is his prophet?" Mr. H. asked.

"It is Mohammed," was the answer.

Said Mr. H., "Mohammed was an impostor, a wicked man, and no prophet; if you trust to him for salvation you will be lost;" whereupon the venerable Mussulman was displeased and looked very sad.

Two of the native Christians are suffering a series of petty persecutions which are very annoying. They have kept very quiet, and are determined to retain their homes and their families, and not be driven forth from them. One evening a number of Mohammedans came with one of the Christians to our house and asked Mr. H. if the man had drunk wine and eaten pork, and so become a Christian. Mr. H. assured them that he was not aware of his having done either of those terrible things, but that he hoped he was a Christian. He then explained to them what it is to be a Christian, and said he wished they might all become Christians immediately. Their temper cooled at once, and when they left they assured Mr. H. that they were delighted with his kindness, and should certainly visit him again.

The school attracted much attention, and had many visitors. The Scripture lessons became very prominent, and were regarded by Mr. H. as a means of great good not only to the scholars, but, indirectly, to their parents.

If my health had been sufficiently good to persevere in the attempt, I have no doubt I should have been able to obtain ingress to many families connected with the school, through the scholars; but I could do nothing more than spend a few hours each day in study and translating, and an hour morning and evening in instructing the five or six children on the premises.

I went one day with Mr. H. to visit the Christian policeman. His house stood upon a high terrace overlooking the street. He brought seats for Mr. H. and himself, but asked me to go in and see his wife. I went in gladly, and found a pleasant young woman, with whom I was soon engaged in conversation. I found she had but little idea of Christianity, except that it is a different belief from Mohammedanism. Of its inward, spiritual nature she had no conception. She said to me that a large family lived next to her, and as they never saw a mem sahib, they would be delighted to have me converse with them a few moments. I signified my willingness to see them, and soon about thirty women and girls made their appearance. The eldest was an aged woman, the great, great grandmother of the young children. She said she was nearly one hundred years old. Poor creature! all those long years she had never heard of the Saviour of sinners! I had an interesting conversation with them, and promised to visit them often; but, alas! the hot wind began to blow, and my health failed so fast that I was obliged to leave these interesting openings for Nynee Tal.

I left Shahjehanpore on the evening of the thirteenth of May, and reached Bareilly the next morning. In consequence of some delay in laying my dak from there to Kaleedoongee, I remained in Bareilly two or three days. By so doing I made the acquaintance of Mr. and Mrs. Jackson, whom I had previously seen for a few hours only as they passed through Shahjehanpore on their way to Bareilly. I found Mrs. Jackson to be one of those amiable spirits that endear themselves to every one with whom they come in contact. It was emphatically true of her that

> "None knew her but to love her,
> None named her but to praise."

The day before I left Bareilly there was a violent storm of wind and rain, which, although it lasted but a short time, did much damage. Thatched buildings were unroofed, and trees broken and uprooted. We rode through cantonments after the storm ceased, and counted over thirty fine trees that were entirely ruined.

I visited the orphanage and spoke with the children, especially with the boys who had been in our care. There was a fine class of these older boys in Mr. Waugh's charge. I heard them recite to him one day, and found they had improved rapidly. Gulab, the famine orphan who came with his brother to us at Budaon, now brought the little fellow forward with great pride, and showed me what a fine strong lad he had become. Poor Gulab! he saw his brother sicken and die that season, and the only ministration that was left him was to plant flowers on his grave.

The night was pleasant during my solitary journey from Bareilly to Rampore; but on the succeeding night, during my journey from that place to Kaleedoongee, there were severe dust storms. The first one came on before midnight, quite suddenly. An immense volume of dust from the west swept over earth and sky, enveloping both in a sable shroud.

My kahars hurried me to a village near the roadside, and carried me, palkee and all, right into the house of a venerable Mussulman who sat on his charpaee (bedstead) in the doorway.

After waiting a long hour, during which the wind blew terrifically, we again ventured to go on. I slept for an hour or two when the kahars wakened me with the intelligence that another dust storm was fast approaching. That time they took me into an open shop that stood by the road. We remained there an hour, and then went on, without much interruption, until we reached Kaleedoongee, where I found a jhaumpaun and bearers which had been sent down from Nynee Tal to take me up.

I reached the mission house at Nynee Tal about four o'clock P. M., and had the pleasure of meeting Mr. and Mrs. Thoburn, whom I had not seen since their marriage.

I found Mrs. Thoburn apparently enjoying good health, and busily engaged in a girls' school. There were thirty names on the roll, with an average attendance of twenty.

The scholars seemed quite in earnest about learning to read, but the chief attraction was crocheting in worsteds. Those who attended regularly received two pice daily. The articles they manufactured, which found a ready sale in Nynee Tal, helped to defray the expense of the school considerably.

Mrs. Thoburn's health began to fail in June, and she was obliged to give up her school duties in consequence. I kept the school up a few weeks with the aid of the catechist's wife, but after the rains fairly set in my health was unequal to the task.

During July and August the rains were almost incessant. Mrs. Thoburn and I were obliged to keep in-doors, and, most of the time, to our couches. I have no doubt the dampness and ill ventilation of the house contributed greatly to our illness.

The last of August there was a slight cessation of the rains, and I seized the opportunity to lay my dak to Shahjehanpore.

My journey home was a series of exposures. Part of the time the rain fell in torrents, and for many a weary mile the water was so deep that the kahars carried the palkee on their shoulders and heads.

I stopped in Bareilly over the Sabbath. Mr. and Mrs. Jackson had just removed to Budaon, and Mr. and Mrs. Thomas had just arrived and were about to take possession of the vacant bungalow. Intelligence had just been received from Lucknow that Mrs. Pierce was lying in a most critical state, and that it was feared she had not long to live.

I reached home on Tuesday morning, and for several weeks suffered extremely from the effects of the journey and the heat. My physician told me that I could not live much longer in this country, and advised me, if I could not go home at once to try a sea voyage, but we could not think the case so desperate as to demand either.

BAREILLY, Nov. 4, 1862.

The fall of 1862 will long be remembered in our mission. On the fifteenth day of September we received a telegram from Mr. Waugh, stating that Mrs. Jackson had been confined of a son on the thirteenth, and that both mother and child had died! There was sincere mourning throughout the mission for Mrs. Jackson. A native Christian woman who knew her well said to me, "We are all sad on account of the death of Jackson mem sahib; she was a true Christian and loved us greatly."

Mrs. Knowles wrote me in regard to her death as follows: "Sister Jackson received the tidings both of her own approaching death and of the departure of her little babe before her, with great calmness. Mr. K. went in to see her ere she left us for heaven, and tried to point her to the precious Jesus and his all-atoning blood, and to the sweet promises of God in Christ. A holy radiance lit up her dying face as she responded, 'Yes, blessed, blessed, blessed promises.' Her soul was resting upon them as upon a rock, and she was happy and fully prepared for the great change. She soon became insensible, and remained so till her death."

Mrs. Thoburn wrote me: "How sad the death of dear Sister Jackson! A purer spirit could not have left our midst. I feel to mourn a sister beloved." Mrs. Jackson left one child, little Bessie, not yet two years old.

As we could not telegraph to Seetapore, we wrote the news of Mrs. Jackson's death to Mr. and Mrs. Gracey. When they received it they were in a very anxious state about Mrs. Parker, who had been taken there by her husband in the hope that a change of air might be beneficial. The rainy season had developed the unhealthiness of Wesleypore most fearfully. The poor Sikhs suffered greatly, and many died, some of them happy in the Lord. Muassee Sing, a catechist, refused to leave when permission was given him unasked, saying he preferred to remain with his people till they could all go together, and if the Lord should call him meanwhile he was ready. He shortly heard the summons, "Come up higher," and died rejoicingly. Mallah, Minepul Sing's wife, also died. Her last words were, "Lord Jesus, receive my spirit."

In the midst of our sicknesses and bereavements have we not abundant encouragement in such deaths?

Mr. and Mrs. Parker, who were living in the village, remained at their post, dealing out medicines and rendering all possible aid, until both were seized with the fever, and Mrs. Parker became so very ill that they were obliged to leave. She recovered slowly; but they are both poorly, and suffer a great deal at times with chills and fever.

Meanwhile the tidings from Lucknow were to the effect that Mrs. Pierce could not long survive. My health improved somewhat, and I exerted myself to revise my latest hymns, as Mr. Waugh wished to get out a small mission hymn book. I succeeded in getting thirty-three ready for the press, which, with seventeen selections (by permission) from the Presbyterian Mission Hymn Book, made us a little book of fifty hymns.

The last week of October was spent in packing our goods, as we had again received marching orders, this time to Moradabad. In the midst of our labors one day, our bearer brought us a telegraphic dispatch that had just been left at the house. "Dear Sister Pierce is gone," I said involuntarily. Mr. H. did not reply, but stood reading the telegram over and over, as if he doubted the evidence of his senses. Finally he said, "No, not Sister Pierce, but Sister Thoburn, died this morning." The shock was so great that I could not speak for a few moments, and my heart seemed to cease beating. I could not realize that she was indeed gone. We knew she had given birth to a son, and was not recovering her health so fast as was desirable, but did not know that she was considered to be in a dangerous state. By a letter received from Mr. Thoburn a few days afterward we learned that her death was most triumphant. "It is sweet to die," was her testimony as she passed through the river to the "beautiful land" she had so long regarded as her home. She lŏved the missionary work, O how intensely! Her labors, amid illnesses and weariness oft, bear witness to her affection for these degraded, these perishing souls. But when she heard the voice of her Saviour calling her to rest and glory, she joyfully obeyed the summons.

> "O may I triumph so,
> When all my warfare's past;
> And, dying, find my latest foe
> Under my feet at last!"

Mr. H. felt the parting from his teachers and scholars in the Shahjehanpore school very much. On the last day he met with them the boys expressed much regret that he was to leave them, and many of the larger ones, some of whom were Mohammedans, wept freely. He rose soon after the midnight preceding our departure, to prepare some papers which he had not been able to write previously, on account of the constant press of work and company, but he had only got well to work when he was interrupted by a low rap at the door, and one of the under teachers of the school came in. He was struggling with deep convictions of duty. He felt convinced that Hindooism is false and Christianity is true, and that he ought to renounce the one and embrace the other; but he did not feel able to meet the remonstrances and persecutions of his friends.

Mr. H. prayed with him, and in the long conversation that ensued, tried to show him the superiority of those things that are not seen, but are forever sure, over those that are temporal and transitory.

The first intelligence we received, when we reached Bareilly, was that Mrs. Pierce was dead. Her death did not take us by surprise, as did the former visits of the dread reaper to our mission; but we all felt that our mission had sustained a great loss in Mrs. Pierce. She had always seemed particularly near to me on account of our long companionship. We had always been sincerely attached to each other, and had kept up a close correspondence until within a few months of her death.

But she has gone to join the bright band on the other shore; gone from her family to whom she was tenderly attached, from the mission circle of which she was a loved and honored member, from the orphan girls who for nearly four years had been the objects of her incessant care and love; but the memory of her beautiful and self-denying life will ever be precious.

Hers was the death of the righteous. Mrs.

Baume, who was with her all through her last sickness, wrote me as follows: "I often thank God for the precious privilege of being with Sister Pierce during her illness, and especially her last days, which were days of triumph in Jesus. She was indeed filled with love, perfect love which casteth out all fear. I said to her, 'Have you any special message for Sister Humphrey?' She answered, 'O tell her to be holy, and do all she can for the poor degraded females of India, but tell her to be very careful of her health and live as long as possible.' These were her messages to all the sisters in the mission, and nothing more."

We shall go on from here to Moradabad in a day or two, and you will hear our report from that place in good time.

LETTER XVIII.

Moradabad — Native Christians — Dr. Mullens — Journey to Lahore — Girls' School — Annual Meeting — Arrangement of Work — Effect of Preaching — Boys' School — Translations — Preparations to return Home — Meela — Interesting Aspect of Native Work—Zhoor-ul-Huqq — Umbeeka Churn.

MORADABAD, Feb. 8, 1864.

MY DEAR MOTHER,—We arrived in Moradabad in due time, and received a real home-like welcome from Joseph Fieldbrave and family, who with the other native Christians was in charge of the mission premises. He had prepared a nice breakfast for us in the dining-room of the mission house, which thoughtful attention was duly appreciated and improved by us.

You perceive from this incident that these people are just like the rest of mankind. False, corrupt systems of belief make men vile, superstitious, and cruel; but the religion of Jesus makes them virtuous, intelligent, and courteous.

We were glad to meet Joseph and his family again, and to have them associated with us, but we were sorry to find Sophia out of health. Rose Anna had changed very much, and had grown to be a pretty-looking, intelligent young woman. Mr. Jackson was stationed here with us, but after three or four weeks he left for Calcutta, in order to send his motherless little Bessie, who was very delicate, to England.

After the usual amount of labor and confusion, we again became settled at our work. We found quite a large boys' school in operation. Besides Joseph, we had Andreas, a catechist from a mission of the Church of England. His wife Priscilla is an amiable, quiet little woman, who sincerely desires to be a humble, useful Christian. He has also a father, brother, sister, and uncle, and these, with two other nominal Christian families that live on the premises, make quite a little community.

There were also three inquirers here when we came; one was an intelligent man of the kyasth, or writer caste, and the other two were priests of the chumar, or shoemaker caste. Mr. H. baptized them a few weeks after our arrival. The kyasth, whose name is Ummed Sing, has some education, and bids fair to become a useful, consistent laborer among the people. The other men did not remain with us long after their baptism, but we hope they will advance steadily in faith and knowledge wherever they are.

Just before Mr. Jackson's departure, we received the very pleasant surprise of a visit from Dr. Mullens, of Calcutta. He was on his way to the hills for a change of air. His talented and devoted wife has been called to her glorious and eternal home. We were much interested in his accounts of her literary labors, and her successful efforts to gain admittance to zenanas. Her books, "Phulmane and Karuna," "What is Christianity," etc., are most interesting. The first named work especially must eventually be a great favorite with native women of all classes. It has been translated into several native dialects.

The zenana mission in Calcutta is of recent date. The mutiny, instead of injuring the cause of Christianity, as its instigators hoped and expected, was used by Him who "turneth the hearts of men as the rivers of water are turned," as a means of advancing public opinion in its favor. Among other subjects, female education came to be regarded with greater complacency. Mrs. Sale, a lady resident of Calcutta, first gained admission to two zenanas, which she visited regularly until her return to England, when Mrs. Mullens, who had just returned from a visit to that country, took them in charge. Soon after a third family was added, and Mrs. Mullens disengaged herself from other duties and prepared to give her whole time to this work. Two other houses near her own residence were opened to her, and letters were received from native gentlemen asking for her services in their families. In a few months she had under visitation and instruction eight zenanas and three girls' schools, containing eighty ladies and seventy girls. She was assisted in this work by native teachers. They visited the scholars daily, while Mrs. Mullens visited every house personally once a week, to give instruction.

Her scholars were taught reading, writing, wool-work, and crochet. Her eldest daughter took charge of the work department, while her own time was devoted exclusively to hearing her scholars' lessons and holding conversations with them. She gave them her own books to read, but did not at first introduce the Bible. Before long, however, the Gospels were given to all that could read, and the teachings and character of our Saviour began to be the frequent subjects of conversation. Meanwhile Miss Sandys and others were successful in gaining admission to native women of the higher classes in the very heart of the city, and had established schools among them.

Mrs. Mullens died very suddenly, soon after the decease of Mr. Lacroix, her gifted and apostolic father. What a happy meeting must theirs have been in that City of Light, "beyond the tide."

The work commenced by Mrs. Mullens is now carried on by her daughter and others in whose hearts God has planted a desire to benefit the women of India.

Soon after the departure of Mr. Jackson,

Mr. Cawdell and family arrived, and occupied half the mission house.

My health improved so fast as the cold season advanced, that I was able to commence a school. Priscilla and Lydia, her sister-in-law, Rose Anna and Piyare, Gungeeah, our sais's daughter, who had not only been kept at her reading, but had been drawn into the Sabbath-school while we were in Shahjehanpore, with two or three others from outside the mission, made up the school, which, although small, was quite as large as I felt able to manage.

The first hour of school was devoted to reading in the Bible, singing, prayers, reciting hymns, catechism, etc. During the second hour reading and writing in English and in the Roman-Oordoo, and reading in Hindee, were taught. The third hour was devoted to knitting and crocheting in wools. I purchased assorted Berlin wools, and taught them to crochet children's socks, mittens, neckties, hoods, etc., and when a dozen or so articles were completed I sent them to the ladies of the station for sale. In this way I paid for the wool, and also gave the girls a fair price for their work.

In December Mr. H. accompanied Dr. Butler and Mr. Hauser to Lahore, to attend a general missionary conference. Lahore is about four hundred miles from Moradabad, in a north-westerly direction.

They visited the cities of Delhi, Umbala, Lodianah, and Kuppurthala on their way. This last is the capital of a small state of the same name, under the dominion of a Sikh rajah who is a Christian in belief, although he has never been baptized. There is a mission at Kuppurthala which is largely supported by the rajah. It was indeed established at his solicitation. One of the missionaries is the Rev. Mr. Woodside, whose acquaintance we made at Dayrah Doon; the other is the Rev. Mr. Newton, M.D. The rajah has provided houses for the missionaries, as well as school buildings and a dispensary, and is building a beautiful church. He is in constant communication with the missionaries, attends their services, and sends his sons to them to be taught. All public work is stopped throughout the estate, on the Sabbath, and thus the rajah's example, as well as the instructions of the missionaries, is brought to bear upon the people. The rajah's present wife is a Christian, the daughter of the English manager of his estates. He was present at the conference, which was largely attended by missionaries from nearly all the Protestant missions in that section of the country.

Questions of deep interest and important bearing upon the missionary work were discussed. The rajah spoke strongly in favor of female education.

At Umbala and Lodianah, as well as at Umritser, which city they visited after leaving Kuppurthala, our party visited the missions, and inspected their schools. At Umbala there is an extensive American Presbyterian mission, a printing press, city school, and girl's orphanage, all of which seemed to be in a flourishing condition.

They also visited the ancient temples and palaces of Delhi, the once famous city of kings, and of the other cities. In Umrister they visited a large establishment for making up the cashmere wool into shawls and cloths.

During the conference week the whole body was invited to several entertainments at the residences of the civilians, and also to a large party given by the rajah of Kuppurthala.

The sacrament of the Lord's Supper was administered to the conference on the evening of the twenty-eighth of December by the Rev. Mr. Janvier.* Seven different denominations, and as many nations, were represented. It was an impressive season.

While Mr. H. was absent I pursued the even tenor of my way, attending to my school and studies. Mr. Cawdell was ill during the time with chills and fever, or, as we call it here, jungle fever, as it is caused by the malaria from the jungles.

* Mr. Janvier has since been murdered by a Hindoo fanatic.

On Christmas day he exerted himself to preach, and we had a pleasant service with the native Christians, interspered with Christmas hymns in Hindoostanee.

During the day the usual "nuzzers" from the city came pouring in, but as it was known that Mr. H. was absent, the donors did not accompany their gifts.

During Mr. H.'s absence I had the pleasure of a visit from Rev. Mr. Sherring and family, of a mission in Benares. They had been spending several months in the hills on account of Mr. Sherring's health.

Soon after Mr. H. returned he visited the Sikh villages, and made arrangements for a school at Babookera, and for religious services to be held regularly there and at Jua, a small village just beyond. Some of the survivors of Wesleypore had returned to their homes, and with other nominal Christians, formed quite a little community.

Ummed Sing was located at Babookera as a teacher.

The first week of February we went over to Bareilly to attend our annual meeting. It was a memorable occasion. A large reinforcement had just arrived, consisting of Dr. and Mrs. Johnson, Mr. and Mrs. Scott, Mr. and Mrs. Mansell and child, Miss White, Miss Porter, and Mr. Wilson.

In the midst of the accumulated business of two years, and the pleasant excitement of meeting each other, we did not forget those who had gone from among us the past year. Mr. Baume gave us a sermon in which he rendered a tribute to their worth, and exhorted us to live in the enjoyment of a like precious faith.

I felt very grateful to my heavenly Father for the privilege of meeting our missionaries at this time. It was a pleasure I scarcely expected to have, and that I knew I might be enjoying now for the last time.

Although my health was greatly improved, yet I knew it was not firmly established, and the coming season might again bring me low.

I was glad to see that most of the missionaries seemed to be in good health, and had a fair prospect of usefulness before them.

Mr. Hicks and his wife were obliged to leave the country on account of the failure of his health. They left during the meeting, bearing with them the sympathies and prayers of all.

I met at this time Mr. and Mrs. Hauser, and Mrs. Messmore, (formerly Miss Husk,) whom I had not previously seen, and I also saw the dear little babe left by Mrs. Thoburn, who is in Mrs. Waugh's charge. Mr. Messmore, Mrs. Baume, and Mrs. Judd were not present. We were, of course, appointed to Moradabad. Mr. and Mrs. Parker were appointed our colleagues,

Mission Cemetery at Nynee Tal.

and so were to continue their work among the Sikhs.

Soon after our return home the remnant of the Wesleypore colony came back to their native villages. We felt a great deal of sympathy for these people, as they had suffered severely. Several of them died on the way to their homes, and others died soon after reaching them. Minepul Sing came back quite out of health. Gurdial was well, and commenced service with us as house bearer at once.

Joseph was removed from Moradabad at the annual meeting, and Zahoor-ul-Huqq and Umbeeka Churn were appointed as our native helpers. The former had taken a wife previously from the Christian village in Bareilly.

Mr. H. went to work with his new staff of helpers with increased energy. Every morning he spent two hours in the school, and after passing the intervening hours until evening in study, writing, etc., he went to the city or to a village to preach. He always called Zahoor-ul-Huqq, Umbeeka Churn, and Andreas into his study before leaving, when they arranged their plan for the preaching, selecting a subject, and each one having a certain phase of it to lay before the people. They then prayed together for the Divine Spirit to accompany the gospel message. The people became aroused and alarmed, and spirited disputations increased upon every successive raid upon their false systems of belief. Often when Mr. H. or Zahoor-ul-Huqq was preaching, a Mohammedan would cry out, "Koran bar-huqq hai, Mohammed sacheha hai;" that is, "the Koran is true, Mohammed is true."

They often asked, "Why do you say so much about Jesus and so little of the other prophets?" whereupon Mr. H. would tell them that Jesus was greater than the prophets, and then give them yet another lesson upon the office and character of our blessed Saviour.

One evening the Mohammedans were more excited than usual, and when the preachers had finished talking and turned to leave the bazar, some one raised the cry, "Mohammed kee deen," that is, "The faith of Mohammed," when instantly it was caught up by scores of "the faithful," accompanied by clappings of the hands, and thus in a most violent and contemptuous manner they followed them out of the city with the din.

I was really frightened when they came home and told of being sent off with such acclaim, and said, "They will murder you some time when they are so excited and angry;" but Mr. H. only laughed, and said they had pretty good evidence that the people understood the preaching and felt the force of the truth.

Mr. H. and Zahoor-ul-Huqq alternated in going out to the Sikh villages once a fortnight.

The school at Babookera prospered well. Ummed Sing was very acceptable to the people and seemed to be doing them good. Zahoor-ul-Huqq remarked of him, "Uska dil saccha hai," that is, "His heart is true."

Mr. Parker, who has tried faithfully to labor both at preaching and in the school, but found his health unequal to such exertion, became so much worse as the hot weather advanced, that it was evident he must go to Nynee Tal. Just before he and his wife left we received a visit from Mr. Woodside, of Kuppurthala. We enjoyed his short stay with us very much.

The boys' school occasioned us much anxiety at one time, as we had not funds sufficient for its support this year. Mr. H. had recourse to his usual expedient for raising funds for such purposes, and was glad to find the English residents in Moradabad as ready and generous in giving aid as those in Bareilly, Budaon, and Shahjehanpore.

The judge and magistrate of the station, after subscribing liberally, sent him word that if more should be needed at any time it should be forthcoming.

It occasions some surprise here, that with such a war in the United States, and consequent financial pressure upon the people, our missionary board can yet sustain its agents in foreign fields.

Mr. H. held a public examination of the school in June. Several of the civilians, as well as native gentlemen, were present, and expressed much pleasure at the efficiency and good management of the school.

When Mr. Parker left for Nynee Tal, Mr. H., with the native helpers, was left to carry on the work alone—the preaching, the school, and the work among the Sikhs. It was evident that all this would be too much for him during the hot season, so, after some preliminary writing, Mr. Mansell, who had been appointed to Lucknow, came to Moradabad.

The hot season soon came on in all its intensity, but the mission house was very comfortable, and we felt the heat less than usual, at least so it seemed to us. But in spite of all our comforts and appliances for coolness, my strength failed in a most unaccountable manner. I gave up my school and tried to save myself, but all was of no avail. A low fever set in, my side became increasingly painful, and my throat and mouth were inflamed and filled with canker, until I could scarcely take food sufficient to sustain life. I finally became so much reduced, that our physician said there was no other chance for life, I must go to Nynee Tal, so with much reluctance we made our preparations for another long separation.

I commenced May in Nynee Tal. The cool

hill climate acted like a charm upon me. In one week after my arrival the fever had left me, and the canker in my throat had disappeared.

I hoped for a while to be able to return to Moradabad immediately after the rains should set in, but I was attacked by my old antagonist, chronic dysentery, and was told by my physician that if I went down into the heat I would probably forfeit my life.

I think if I had occupied dry, comfortable rooms all the time I was in Nynee Tal I might have been spared the severe sickness that followed; but the mission house was crowded, and part of the time some were not accommodated even so well as I was.

My room was dark, damp, and poorly ventilated, and, although there was a fireplace, a fire was an impossibility on account of the smoke. The last of June my health failed so fast that my physician said I must have better rooms if possible.

I removed accordingly, and took up my quarters in two small, but very comfortable rooms in the wing of a house occupied by Dr. Butler and family, but the change was too late to avert the consequences of former exposure.

I was taken very ill, and grew worse so rapidly that Mr. H., who had but just returned home after making me a short visit, came up again in great haste, fearing it was to see me die.

I thought myself at one time that I might soon be laid by Mrs. Thoburn in our lovely cemetery on the hill-side, but it was our Father's will and good pleasure to raise me up again.

Through July and August Mr. H. remained by me, and I have no doubt his care contributed in a great measure to my recovery. But my system was so debilitated that I could no longer rally as heretofore, and it soon became evident that unless a great change should take place we must indeed return home for a while. We did not wish to do this, however, unless there were a fair prospect that by doing so my health might be restored. I have no wish to return home to die, I would much rather die in India.

We consulted several physicians, who gave it as their opinion that I might regain my health in our home climate, and be enabled to return to our work in India. Under these considerations we applied to our missionary board for leave to return home.

Mr. H. returned to Moradabad the last of August, but I remained a month longer. Mrs. Hauser and her little daughter were with me, which prevented me from being lonely. I was able to study and translate a little every day, and began my walks and rides again about the hills. I even began to cherish the hope that we might after all remain at our work.

But during the journey down from the hills

I met with a long detention on account of the breaking of my jhaumpaun, during which I caught a severe cold. Soon after my arrival home I was again seized with low fever and pain in my side, which, instead of being temporary as heretofore, has never left me wholly during the season.

It seemed hard not to be able to reopen my school nor to visit the Sikh villages, as I hoped to do these pleasant months. I feel particularly interested in these people, as we have free access to their families, and the young women and girls among them are generally anxious to learn.

O how I longed for strength to go among them and tell them of my Saviour and theirs, and teach them to read his word. But now that I had attained sufficient fluency in the language to do this with ease, my strength would not admit of the exertion. So I gave my attention, whenever I was able to do anything, to what I could do, namely, to instructing the Christian and Sikh women on the mission premises and to translating.

During the year I gathered some fugitive translations of previous years, and prepared them for the press in the form of a small book, entitled "Akhlaqi Kahanian," that is, Moral Stories. There were ten in all. Seven of them were gleaned from the "Ladies' Repository" and the "Northern Christian Advocate," and the others were the first three chapters of Dr. Wise's "Precious Lessons." To each of the stories I added a few stanzas. It is being published in Roman-Oordoo.

I also translated a beautiful allegory, called "The White Dress," from an English publication. It is being published in Persi-Arabic, in tract form. I succeeded, too, in translating several hymns, which brought the number, including those already published, to sixty.

While I am truly grateful that God enabled me to do even this work, I am not blind to the fact that these translations are necessarily imperfect, and will doubtless soon be superseded by worthier productions.

Still, there must be a beginning, and I am glad to have contributed my mite to it. I sincerely hope there will be great and rapid progress in these and all matters pertaining to our work, and if it please God to grant me an opportunity to share in it I shall be most thankful.

In November Mr. Mansell and Mr. Humphrey, accompanied by Zahoor-ul-Huqq and Andreas, visited the great annual Ganges mela at Ghurmuckteeser, about forty miles distant from Moradabad. They pitched their tent on a reserved space occupied by the police, having obtained permission of the officer present to do so.

The mela was attended by a vast multitude, estimated at about one hundred thousand. The people arranged rude tents in streets, where they ate and slept. During the day they first bathed in the Ganges and celebrated pooja, after which they assembled in groups to listen to the vagaries of the priests, jugglers, and dancing girls.

Some shrewd ones drove bargains at some of the numerous stalls, where fabrics and wares of native manufacture were displayed in abundance.

As the sun declined, the rajahs and raees who were present paraded the streets on richly caparisoned elephants and horses, and the entire male portion of the assemblage, in their gayest apparel, either joined the motley procession, or formed groups of entranced admirers of the show. Music of course held a prominent place in the entertainment. The Hindoos think they have a peculiar faculty for producing sweet sounds, and say that although the English surpass them in most things, they cannot go beyond them in music!

They allow their women to be present at these gatherings, but the purdah or curtain is not left behind. The high caste women, closely covered with their chudders, keep in the background at the public exhibitions, and at other times remain in their tents.

Of course these melas furnish fine opportunities for sowing the good seed of the kingdom broadcast, both by preaching and distribution of books, as the people are away from their business and have leisure to see and hear.

At this mela the people listened attentively, and frequently opened discussions which showed that they understood what was said to them. One brahmin thought that every religion was good and would save all who believed in it. Another wished to know if all that worshiped God would not be saved, intending of course to affirm that all Hindoos did so. Mr. H. told him that all depended upon the spirit in which the worship was rendered, etc., etc.

After the preaching one day a young pundit asked for one of the Gospels, which was given him. He seemed very well disposed, but as soon as he had received the book he shouted out derisively, "Gunga kee jai," that is, victory belongs to the Ganges. The multitude joined instantaneously, and the air was rent with deafening shouts, "Gunga kee jai, Gunga kee jai!"

The months of December and January were spent by the missionaries in the school and city work, and an occasional tour into the district. They visited the Sikh villages several times, and baptized at one time six adults and eight children.

The work among the Sikhs seemed to be prospering well. Minepul Sing had begun the practice of calling his neighbors together at eventide and reading the Bible and praying with them.

At the city of Sambhal they met with a very kind reception from the tehsildar in charge of the pergunna of Sambhal. This native gentleman, who is a frequent visitor at the mission house, supports a school in Sambhal taught by a Hindoo, formerly one of the pupils of the mission school in Moradabad. It was told us that this teacher upon removing his family to Sambhal broke up his household gods and cast them away, saying he would have no more of such nonsense.

The tehsildar wants a Christian teacher, and as soon as one can be spared from the mission he will be located there, and will take charge of the school.

The Hindoos have a tradition regarding Sambhal that the last and holiest incarnation will take place there, and this event is constantly expected.

As the time drew near for our annual meeting in Bareilly, when we were to leave India and turn our faces homeward, the work in Moradabad seemed to increase in interest daily. It is perhaps true that "blessings brighten as they take their flight;" certainly to us the missionary work never seemed so dear as it has this season.

Our relations with the people are most pleasing. There are frequent visitors and inquirers who seem almost ready to embrace Christianity. The natives indeed seem to regard us as their friends, and come to us often for advice and sympathy in their troubles.

The school is in a high state of efficiency and prosperity. Government grants were made this year to several of our mission schools, and among them one of eighty rupees per month to the school in Moradabad.

It was gratifying to us to have Zahoor-ul-Huqq and Umbeeka Churn associated with us this last year of our stay, and to witness their consistent walk and usefulness.

Zahoor-ul-Huqq is a good preacher, quiet and candid, but bold and zealous in the discharge of his duty. He is a good singer, and many a night his voice, tuned to our own hymns, was the latest sound that fell upon our ears. The native Christians' houses stand very near our own, and we could hear their voices very distinctly in the still night.

Umbeeka Churn was converted a Methodist in its true signification, that is, an earnest Christian. He sometimes frightens the people in the bazars, by preaching to them in terrific strains of the sure wrath of God that shall be poured out upon those nations who will not forsake their idolatry and seek the living and true God. He prays with power, and those who listen are convinced that he is in earnest, that he feels his need of the blessings he asks. His voice is heard in the morning usually before any one else on the premises has risen, calling upon God in prayer. He was married in October last to Ellen, the eldest of our orphan girls. She is an intelligent, pious young woman of pleasing manners. We trust they will both be very useful laborers in this great and blessed work.

I was not able to attend the annual meeting, and thus I lost the privilege of seeing the dear band of missionaries again before leaving. Mr. H. went over to Bareilly, but could not remain till the close of the meeting, as our passage was engaged in the screw steamer Golden Fleece, which was advertised to sail on the seventeenth of February.

The members of the mission gave us many assurances of their affection and sympathy. How near they seem to us, and how strong and blessed are the ties that unite our hearts.

May the choicest blessings of heaven be richly shed upon this little band of reapers, and may they gather many sheaves, from the whitening fields around them, into the garner of our Lord!

LETTER XIX.

Parting with Native Christians — Journey to Calcutta — Screw Steamer Golden Fleece — Madras — Illness — Cape of Good Hope — Equator—Fright—Land's End — England — Ireland — Atlantic — New York.

NEW YORK, June 8, 1864.

MY DEAR MOTHER,—On the morning of the tenth of February we gathered in the parlor of the mission house at Moradabad to hold our last religious services with our Hindoostanee brethren and sisters. Minepul Sing and his newly-married wife and sister had walked twenty miles on the previous evening in order to see us before we left, and now his wife wished to be baptized. It was very pleasing to us that this rite should be performed at our parting interview.

After the baptism Mr. H. addressed the little company a few moments, then read and prayed. We sang a hymn together, and then we bade them each and all good-by. I shall never forget that scene. How exceedingly precious those few disciples of our Lord seemed to us as we gazed upon them, perhaps for the last time, and commended them to the care of the "Good Shepherd." The tears coursed down their cheeks freely as they assured us they should not cease to pray that my health might be restored, and we be able to return to them soon.

We traveled by horse dak to Allyghur, which we reached the next morning, after a day and night of excessive fatigue.

From Allyghur we took the cars for Allahabad. Western civilization is indeed making great changes in India, and western Christianity should be advancing more rapidly.

We found Allahabad so much improved as almost to rival the "City of Palaces" itself. Where desert-like sand plains met the eye in 1858, stately dwellings and public buildings had risen as if by magic; and on the spot where we took the cars in March of that year, stood a fine large station house. The seat of government for the Northwest provinces has been changed from Agra to Allahabad, which partly accounts for the change in the appearance of the place.

We stopped through the day at one of the splendid hotels which stand near the station, and at early evening left in a dak garee for Benares.

The railway bridge across the Jumna is in process of erection, and when it is completed there will be no such break in the journey to Calcutta. The line of railway keeps to the south of the Ganges, and thus does not intersect Benares; but a branch runs up to that city, the station of which is just opposite on the southern bank of the river.

We arrived in Benares on Saturday, and remained over the Sabbath at the house of the Rev. Mr. Sherring, of the London Missionary Society mission in that city.

We attended service in the mission chapel on Sabbath morning, and heard Mr. Sherring preach. He speaks the Hindoostanee language very fluently, and it was a pleasure to hear him.

There was a fine congregation of native Christians and scholars from the mission schools. At a service held later in the day Mr. H. preached. In the evening some other missionaries called, and Mr. Sherring and Mr. Humphrey accompanied them to a general missionary prayer meeting.

Early on Monday morning Mr. Sherring took us in his carriage across the Ganges to the station house.

The cars on the Indian railway are in compartments, as they are in England. We were so fortunate as to have a compartment to ourselves, and Mr. H. was thus enabled to arrange a comfortable place for us to rest during the night.

Tuesday morning, the sixteenth, we arrived in Calcutta, and soon after leaving the train at Howrah, we saw Mr. Young advancing to meet us. How the sight of him recalled our arrival in 1857, and our life in Calcutta. One other kind friend of those days, Mr. Stewart, has returned to Scotland.

We learned from Mr. Young that we must go on board the Golden Fleece that night, so we had only a few hours in which to make the necessary arrangements for the voyage. It was a busy day, but, with Mr. Young's assistance, we were ready in time.

We drove down to Garden Reach about sunset, and once more went on board a dinghy. We found that the Golden Fleece had dropped down the river some distance, and we had a long row in prospect to reach her.

Mr. Young accompanied us, and thus the first friendly face we met upon our arrival in India was also the last we gazed upon when we left her shores. We bade him good-by in the saloon of the steamship, and then slightly arranged our cabin and retired for the night, but not to sleep. The night was unusually sultry for that season. The jackals had not forgotten how to make "night hideous" by their "sylvan strains." Passengers were continually arriving, children crying, and the nurses making drowsy and worse than useless attempts to quiet them.

In the morning at breakfast we met our fellow-passengers, but the officers were not present. There were, including ourselves, fourteen adults and twelve children.

Three ladies were going to England on account of ill-health, leaving their husbands in India; and one entire family, also on account of disease. One single lady, a Miss Rocke, was returning from a visit to some friends. The complement was made up of young officers who were returning either on account of ill-health or ill-conduct. Of the former number was a son of General Neil.

The Golden Fleece is an iron ship of two thousand seven hundred tons burden. She is a full-rigged sailing vessel with a small steam power attached, which is sufficient to take her along at the rate of seven knots an hour in calms and variable winds.

We glided easily down the Hooghly, over the bars and sands that caused so much alarm in the Niobe, and long before evening the last point of Saugur island disappeared from our sight.

With far greater regret than when the shores of our native land faded from our view, we asked ourselves, "Shall we never look upon these shores again?"

Captain Bird, the commander of the ship, is a fine-looking gentleman past the prime of life. He is a member of the Church of England, and believes in keeping up at least the forms of religion. He desired Mr. H. to always ask a blessing at dinner, and to read the Church service and preach a short sermon on deck every Sabbath morning.

The rules of the ship were very strict in regard to the Sabbath. The decks were scrubbed every morning except on that day, and they were washed twice on Saturday. All the sailors except those on duty were required to be cleanly dressed and marched forward to the seats arranged for them. The capstan, which served for a pulpit, was always covered with the British flag. There was a large awning over a portion of the deck, which made it a comfortable place to sit.

We anchored off Madras on the Saturday evening after sailing, and remained there till the sixth of March, in order to take on board cargo and passengers.

There is no bay at Madras. The ocean waves break with full force upon the beach, and are crested with snow-white and angry-looking surf through which ordinary boats cannot pass. The natives have contrived peculiar boats, the planks of which are fastened together with strong cords yielding somewhat to the action of the waves. They are called Masulah boats, and are always used for the transportation of cargoes and passengers to and from the ships. We saw also very singular-looking crafts, apparently made of a single plank, or half the trunk of a tree, bearing one man each. They are called catamarans.

Our vessel was besieged with boats filled with dealers in fruit, ornaments, curiosities, embroideries, silks, etc. Among them were silk robes embroidered with cotton, and the most exquisite embroidered muslins and laces I ever saw.

Most of the passengers went ashore at Madras; but the ladies were so utterly terror-stricken, and told of such marvelous escapes, that I concluded to remain quietly on board. Mr. H., however, went ashore twice and looked about the city, and visited the Rev. Dr. Winslow and Mr. Hunt of the mission of the American Board. There were some other American missionaries there from a station some distance in the country, and one of them accompanied Mr. H. to the ship and made me a short visit.

A crowd of people came on board at Madras, so that when we left we had nearly a hundred adult passengers and forty children. There were over one hundred and thirty of the ship's crew, which made the whole number of souls on board about two hundred and seventy.

The weather was intensely hot while we were off Madras. I was taken very ill the day before we sailed, and for two weeks was confined wholly to my berth. Some of the time it seemed doubtful if I could rally; but in two or three weeks, as we gained the colder latitudes, I began to recover. As soon as I was a little stronger, the physican ordered me to be carried out daily to the sofa of the stern window for fresh air, and many an hour I lay there quaffing the pure sea breezes and watching the heaving sea.

As the stern window was a favorite resort for the lady passengers, I made their acquaintance under rather disadvantageous circumstances; but before we had been a month out from Madras, I was able to resume my seat at table and mingle with the passengers.

One gentleman, who came on board at Madras quite out of health, died in about three weeks, and was buried in the ocean.

Among the passengers were a general and his family going home to England for life, with whom we formed a very pleasant acquaintance. Perhaps one reason we liked them so well was that they sympathized with the North in the great struggle for the right.

Several of the company asked Mr. H. to conduct an evening service on the Sabbath, and also to have prayers every morning in the saloon. After consulting Captain Bird and finding he had no objections, he consented to do so, and throughout the voyage he held two services on the Sabbath and morning prayers throughout the week.

There was a piano on board, and as there were several good players and singers, the hymns and chants were rendered in good style, and added very much to the interest of the services.

Off Mauritius and Madagascar the weather was cold and squally, but we had no severe storms. As we rounded the Cape of Good Hope, we met heavy seas that made our good ship tremble. There had evidently been a tempest, and the waves had not yet subsided. The wind was fair, and we plowed through the advancing billows at a fearful rate.

When we got into the current off Point Agulhas, which took us along at the rate of four knots an hour, we were making thirteen by our sails; and seventeen miles an hour made even the Golden Fleece "reel to and fro and stagger like a drunken man."

The night previous to our reaching Cape Town the phosphorus in the water was magnificent: the waves "mountain high," and the whole vast expanse, far as the eye could reach, gleamed with red light, and on, and on, right through the blazing element, our good ship plowed her way unharmed. I am sure none of us can ever forget the sublimity and supernatural beauty of that scene.

Captain Bird was running for a prize. Five hundred pounds sterling extra were to be his if he made the voyage from Madras to Cape Town in thirty days, and thence to England in forty days. We barely succeeded in casting anchor in Table Bay on the evening of the fifth of April, which was reckoned to be just within the fixed time.

Next morning the bold green mountains of the Cape loomed majestically up before us. As we could not discern them the previous night, the change seemed almost magical. In the center stands Table Mountain, so called from its flat top, which is three miles across. When the storm cloud lowers, it falls down the sides of Table Mountain in such a manner as to gain from mariners the cognomen of "The Tablecloth."

There are two other large mountains, one on either side, with conical peaks and green grassy slopes; but the three mountains are not beautified very abundantly with trees.

At their foot lies Cape Town. Its home-like houses and churches form a very agreeable view to the eyes of voyagers from the East, and very pleasant to the taste are the apples, pears, and grapes, which are abundant at this season of the year.

Excellent wine is made at Constantia, a vineyard but a few miles from the town, and a large supply was taken on board by our fellow-passengers.

Mr. H. went ashore several times, but I only succeeded in getting on deck once, the first time since leaving Madras. We would have enjoyed

18

a few days on shore to visit the missions, etc. We had hoped to meet Dr. Duff at the Cape, as we knew he was making a stay there on his way to Scotland, but he had gone inland a few miles.

Some of the missionaries hearing of us, kindly sent us an invitation to visit them, but we did not receive it in time to do so. About fifteen passengers, adults and children, came on board at Cape Town.

The climate of the Cape must be very like home, although not so severe. We learned from the passengers that snow falls occasionally during three months of the year, June, July and August, but never to any great depth.

I should suppose it would be a better climate for invalids from India to recruit in than that of America or England, and what a saving of time, money, and exposure it would be if missionaries could avail themselves of it. How gladly would we have been spared the remainder of the voyage, if we could have remained there and been comfortably situated.

We were told that before the Overland Route shortened the journey to England, the East India Company sent all its invalids there to recruit.

We sailed on the tenth, and with favoring winds made our way rapidly toward the Equator. As we neared it the wind left us, and we steamed for a week; then again we depended upon our sails. How different from our voyage out! Then we lay becalmed for weeks in the torrid zone, now we had only a week of hot weather.

When off the coast of Guinea we had quite a fright. The funnel burned out one Sabbath evening. We were drinking tea in the saloon, when we heard confused noises overhead, and looking up saw a shower of sparks falling down the main hatchway!

The awning caught fire, and the lower sails were endangered. The ropes which fastened the awning were cut in order to remove it more speedily, and in a short time the danger was averted.

On the eighteenth of May we sighted Land's End, the point where Charles Wesley is said to have composed,

> "Lo! on a narrow neck of land
> 'Twixt two unbounded seas I stand," etc.

It was a time of thrilling excitement to all, especially so to those whose homes were near.

We took a pilot off Plymouth the next morning. On the succeeding night Captain Bird retired, leaving the ship in his charge. Toward morning an invalid gentleman passenger was restless, and rose and went on deck. He observed something just ahead that looked like land, and at once called an officer, who no sooner saw it than he shouted an order to turn the ship about. We were driving right ashore, and so near had we approached, that in turning the ship the proximity to land was hazardous. We were greatly shocked in the morning when we learned what danger we had escaped. The pilot was put off the next day and another taken on board.

Early on the morning of the twenty-third we were all astir gazing on the "white cliffs of Albion," which, in the vicinity of Dover, present a very imposing appearance. We could see the town and the renowned Castle of Dover quite distinctly.

On this, the last morning of our remarkably pleasant voyage, we all met for prayers as usual. Just as they were concluded, Mrs. Cotton, a most lovely and amiable Christian lady, remarked that the lady passengers had deputed her to thank Mr. H. for what they were pleased to term the kind and acceptable manner in which he had conducted religious services on board, and announced that a Bible and Prayer Book would be presented to him in London "as a token of regard, and in remembrance of his kind services." She added that they should always regard our companionship on board with much pleasure, and that it was the wish of all that we might be blessed and prospered in our visit to our native land, and be enabled to return to our work in India. This incident took us by surprise, but was no less grateful to our feelings.

We steamed up the Thames to Gravesend, where most of the passengers left the ship. We were all glad that the voyage was over, and yet there were many regretful feelings that we must now part with but very little prospect of meeting again in this world.

We had become much interested in several of the passengers, especially in Miss Rocke, Mrs. Cotton, and others. Mrs. Thompson, of Cape Town, an estimable Christian lady, seemed like a mother to us. She was on a visit to England and Ireland with her son and daughter. When we landed at Gravesend, they, with us, joined Mr. Fletcher's family party, who were intending to take rooms at Ship Hotel, Charing Cross. After a slight detention at the custom-house we took a cab to the railway station.

How delicious was the land-breeze as we drove along! and how lovely were the lilacs blossoming up against the pleasant English homes! How delightful it was again to glide swiftly along the iron track!

We entered London, vast London, in the evening, and at nine o'clock were taking tea together in a private parlor at Ship Hotel.

It was very pleasant to have the company of these fellow-voyagers while in London. Several others called on us at the hotel, and among them came Judge Cotton with the ladies' remembrancer, a beautiful Bible and Prayer Book, with the names of the donors written on a blank leaf inside, and Mr. Humphrey's name in gilt letters on the outside of each book.

Our friend, Miss Rocke, called and generously gave us ten sovereigns, equal to fifty dollars in gold, for our missionary treasury. Mrs. Thompson also gave us three sovereigns for the same purpose.

As we had but three days in which to make our preparations for the remaining voyage, we had not much opportunity for sight-seeing. For my part, I was so fatigued that I was quite satisfied with what we saw from our parlor windows. Westminster Abbey was close by, and near us, standing by a fountain in full play, was a full size equestrian statue.

The shops opposite the hotel were resplendent with richly-hued fabrics, the sidewalks were crowded with well-dressed people, and the streets with beautiful carriages.

Mr. H. visited City Road Chapel and Wesley's house and tomb, and explored the subterranean railroad which tunnels the great city.

We fully intended to see the interior of Westminster Abbey the day we left London, but when we had walked around the venerable pile and were about to enter, we found the evening service was just commencing, and if we went in we could not leave until it should conclude, and as we had but two hours in which to bid our friends good-by and reach the station, we dared not risk the detention.

We had a charming bird's-eye view of the mother country as on the fleet wings of steam we sped across the country to Liverpool. Two points in relation to Euglish scenery will ever be distinct in my memory. One is the absence of the unsightly board and rail fences which mar the beauty of our home scenery; and, second, the intense green of the landscape. The smooth cosy meadows, with the enclosing hedges, the shrubs, the trees, all are of the deepest richest green.

We saw many of the "stately homes of England" as well as the "cottage homes," standing embowered in groves, and looking the very personification of home comfort. Still I think many parts of our own fair land rival England in this respect, while in extended and varied scenery it, of course, far surpasses her.

We reached Liverpool at eleven o'clock P. M., and went to Queen's Hotel, as we had been advised by our London friends. In about half an hour we were sitting in a nicely furnished room far up skyward, with steaming tea, hot muffins, etc., before us. Really, English hotels are marvelously comfortable places for tired travelers.

On entering the breakfast room next morning we were shown to one of the many small tables that filled the room, where we were served to a delicious breakfast.

We drove through the busy streets of Liverpool for an hour before we made our way to the docks. At one o'clock we went on board the steamer Etna, and glided down the Mersey.

Immediately we found ourselves among our own people once more. Two young gentlemen, two young ladies, and a missionary from Turkey, formed, with ourselves, the American party, which was enlarged at times by sundry others who claimed the United States as their adopted home.

We were a mixed multitude on board the Etna. There were about eighty cabin passengers and six hundred emigrants. All the latter, and some of the former, came on board at Queenstown, Ireland, where we stopped for a few hours.

We saw there the ill-fated "City of York," lying helplessly on the rock which stopped her course forever. It seems that the captain of the unfortunate vessel attempted to pass between the rock and the shore, in order to save a few moments of time, and being deceived by the apparent nearness of the shore in the moonlight, did not allow the rock sufficient latitude. She struck on it, and could not be got off.

All the passengers were saved, but of course they were much terrified, and sustained great loss.

When we left Queenstown, and were fairly out to sea, we began to feel impatient for the first time during the entire journey. Home seemed so near, and yet so far away.

The voyage to New York was only twelve days in length; but O what tedious days they were! Sea-life became almost intolerable, and it was only when we thought of the poor emigrants below, stowed in like baggage as they were, that our own close quarters seemed endurable.

We had gray lowering weather all the way over, but no storm.

On the two Sabbaths we had religious services. Mr. Walker, the missionary from Turkey, preached on one Sabbath and Mr. H. on the other, after the reading of the Church service by the physician on board.

The second Saturday evening a lamentable accident occurred. A young German woman fell down the ladder which led below, and ruptured a blood vessel. She died in a few minutes. On Sabbath morning she was placed in a coffin and cast out into the broad Atlantic.

Just before midday a large ship bore down toward us and signaled us to stop. Our captain declared he would not, and went below; but he had scarcely reached his room when a shot came darting over the water toward us.

There was no escape, we must stop and learn the will of the stranger, so with an ill grace the captain gave the necessary orders to stop the steamer.

The strange vessel, a splendid man-of-war in full sail, bore down so closely that it seemed as if she meant to crush us; but she merely ascertained who we were, and then, without deigning to answer our question, "What is the news?" made off.

Sabbath evening a heavy fog came on, and all night long the portentous fog-bell rang out its warning peals. Toward noon on Monday the fog cleared away, and when the bay, with its lovely islands and stately cities met our gaze, the bright sunshine beamed forth.

Just as we left the steamer, however, clouds overspread the sky, and amid pouring rain we landed, stopped at the custom-house, bade our little party of friends good-by, entered a carriage, and drove to the missionaries' home, the house of the kind and excellent Recording Secretary of the Missionary Board, Rev. D. Terry.

It seems like a dream that we are here again in New York, and that in a few days we shall mingle with the friends we thought never to see again in the flesh.

We do not have a single thought that our

work in India is done. We consider that we are merely home "on furlough," and soon as the purpose for which we returned shall be accomplished, we will gladly return to "the front," if God permit us.

My health is much improved, and we have strong hope that we have yet many years before us to labor in heathen India.

APPENDIX.

THERE were a few errors in the manuscript of this work which I would have corrected in the proofs, but I did not receive them in time to make the necessary alterations; I therefore note them here.

On page 61 the Soane river is said to be "but a rivulet" in the dry season; but instead of this being the case, it is broken into several shallow streams, which thread the deep yellow sand of the bed of the river, which is over three miles wide. While on our journey from Calcutta to Nynee Tal in 1858, we crossed the Soane in the night, and, in fact, did not *see* it at all. Our kahars complained of the deep sand, but said there was very little water.

On page 60 a sufficiently clear idea of the Vindhya Hills is not given. The Vindhyan range comprises all the mountains and hills between the twenty-second and twenty-fifth parallels of latitude, from Guzerat on the west to the Ganges; but the first hills north of Calcutta are usually termed the Bahar Hills, because they are in the province of Bahar. The fact is not mentioned, either, that the singular ledge of rocks called "Adam's Bridge," which connects the two small islands of Rameserum and Manar, in a direct line between the continent and Ceylon, is supposed by the Hindoos to be the remains of the bridge which was constructed by the apes for the recovery of the goddess Seeta.

On page 72, also, in the description of the "Taj Mahal," the impression is given that the whole of the Koran is inlaid upon the walls in precious stones; but this is not so; the letters are formed of black marble. The *Sarcophagi* are inlaid with precious stones, and so are the other portions of the edifice, as mentioned. The description is, however, very incomplete, owing to the little time we had to examine it.

The best description of the Taj Mahal extant, at least in this country, is in Bayard Taylor's "India, China, and Japan," but even that usually correct writer falls into a very great mistake in regard to the personage for whom the mausoleum was erected. He says: "The history and associations of the Taj are entirely poetic. It is a work inspired by love and consecrated to beauty. Shah Jahan, the 'Selim' of Moore's poem, (The Light of the Haram, in Lalla Rookh,) erected it as a mausoleum over his queen, Noor Jahan, the light of the world, whom the same poet calls Noor Mahal, the light of the haram, or, more properly, palace. She is reputed to have been a woman of surpassing beauty, and of great wit and intelligence."

Now Moore himself declares his hero to be "the magnificent son of Akbar," in the opening lines of "The Light of the Haram," and also states in the margin that his name was Selim, but at his coronation he assumed the title of Jahangeer, or Conqueror of the World, which is also an historical fact. The favorite sultana of Jahangeer, whom he named first Noor Mahal, and afterward Noor Jahan, survived him several years, and at her death, in 1646, was buried in a tomb which she had herself erected close to that of Jahangeer at Lahore.*

Khoorum, the favorite son of Jahangeer, (but not the son of Noor Mahal,) was crowned soon after his father's death, and the title of Shah Jahan, or King of the World, was conferred upon him. He built the Taj Mahal in memory of his favorite wife, Mumtaz Mahal, that is, the Chosen of the Palace, and was afterward buried by her side in the vault of that inimitable structure.

E. J. H.

* See "British Possessions in Asia," by R. Montgomery Martin, Esq.

THE END.